zuckerbook

Jerry Zucker Middle School of Science
The Zuckerbook Project
Fall 2021

Faculty Advisor
Mr. Erik J. Hilden

Copy Editing
Erik J. Hilden editor-in-chief
Paiton Garcia Linarte copy editor
Lliana Bomenech copy editor
Jeffrey Mueller copy editor

Art Department
Ka'Naisha Green creative director
Gabby Myers production artist & illistrator
Micayah Seabrook production artist & illustrator

Social Media
Oliva Reyes Arreola social media lead
Esence Richardson social media

Marketing
Brooke Cumbee marketing lead
Miguel Ramirez fundraising
Julia Rodriguez fundraising

Cover Art **Janell Thomas**

© 2021-2022 by **The Zuckerbook Project** in concert with:

The Students of Jerry Zucker Middle School of Science
6401 Dorchester Road, Room 159
North Charleston, South Carolina 29418
Principal: Christopher Haynes
Assistant Principal: Andrea Gadsden
Assistant Principal: Shorace Guider
They are our heroes.

ISBN: 978-0-578-39530-2

Printed in the United States of America.

Dedication

This work is dedicated to the students
who created each piece that is contained
within these pages.
Their words, their art, their spirits,
and their energies bring this work to life.
May their voices always be heard.

Community Involvement

Endeavors such as these are evidence of the great things that can happen when a community pulls together in the face of adversity and produces a testament to the voices of their children. Without the support of our community, this would not have been possible, and without further support, future endeavors may not come to pass. We have had a lot of support this year, but we can always use more, as is true of any non-profit activity. If you are interested in donating to The Zuckerbook Project or are interested in volunteering to help in any way, please feel free to get in touch. I can be reached at **erik_hilden@charleston.k12.sc.us** or at the following address:

The Zuckerbook Project c/o
Jerry Zucker Middle School of Science
6401 Dorchester Rd. Room 159
North Charleston, SC 29418
843-767-8383 ext. 25614
or 503-778-0393. We look forward to hearing from you.

Acknowledgements

Each year, it seems, there are developments, advancements, setbacks, more setbacks, more advancements, and a lot of folly, and every year these fine students and this learning community do not fail to amaze me.

We had a leaner crew for Volume 12. No less dedicated, no less interested, and no less inspired, they worked tirelessly until everything shut down due to the COVID-19 Pandemic and ensuing quarantine. Then I had to pick up the pieces.

Community support is growing and it is that support that is bringing this project to your hands right now. Without our continuing supporters, none of this would be possible, but without our new supporters, we wouldn't be able to reach new heights. In their own way, everyone in this building, as well as people thousands of miles away, has made it possible to continue our work and break new ground.

These fine folks warrant special mention for their continuing support and dedication to the love of reading and writing.

Mr. Christopher Haynes has now joined our ranks and taken the captain's chair at Zucker Middle School and has expressed support for our continued efforts in the Wonderful World of Independent Self-Publishing. Thank you, sir, for the support. We look forward to working with you.

Ms. Erin Presto, 7th grade ELA and Honors ELA teacher, has funneled us talent, art work, and writing. Her involvement and support has been amazing. It is always great to have allies on staff, and Ms. Presto is right at the top of that list. A dear friend and confidante, it is hard to imagine Zucker Middle School without her, or Zuckerbook without her help. Thank you, Erin.

Ms. Mitchell, our new art teacher, jumped right in and funneled a lot of excellent artwork our way, having taken over the art room under duress. Her students are keeping the high standards set by her predecessors and we could not be more pleased. Many of their pieces of art are in this volume. Thank you so much for your support, Ms. Mitchell, and welcome aboard!

The entire faculty and staff of Zucker Middle School has continued to tolerate our pleas for donations and financial support. We are fortunate, indeed, and could not ask for a more supportive community at this school. Thank you. You are appreciated more than you will ever know.

Dr. Clark G. Hilden, who has continued to donate to our cause, deserves special mention, for donating large amounts of money and inspiration, support for our students, and mentoring as we go forward in the unchartered waters of small batch publishing. Take a look at his textbook, ***Uniquely Oregon***, if you want an interesting read about a fascinating state created by a dedicated teacher of geography. It is fun to read regardless of your interests, and available at Amazon.com.

Ms. Rhea Farmer made donations through GoFundMe.com. It is a wonderful thing when the community at large jumps in to assist student projects and support student literacy. Thank you very much for donating! Rhea has been a trusted friend of mine for over fifty years. Just saying that out loud in my mind makes me feel old.

Mr. James Brooks retired at the end of the 2016-2017 school year and is sorely missed. His support for The Zuckerbook Project was unwaivering, and his assistance in assembling the best crew possible for each year was invaluable in setting the standards for this class and this publication. We remain in his debt and envious of his retirement.

Ms. Jordane Lotts and **Ms. Patricia Szczygiel** have taken over the guidance department and have continued working with us to populate our crew with engaged, intelligent, and creative young minds who want to make a difference. Thank you both for your involvement. In the face of changing times and changing norms, we managed to pull it off, and your continued support of what we do is a big reason we continue to succeed. Thank you to both of you.

Ms. Gina Harris and **Mr. Mike Harris** have repeatedly taken it upon themselves to promote The Zuckerbook Project by traveling the world and snapping prictures of Zuckerbook in the hands of children. A trip to Guatemala had them leave a copy in the hands of a young boy whose father began to teach him English by reading Zuckerbook. There are pics of Zuckerbook in Paris, in Pakistan, and all over the place. Unbelievable. Thank you.

Ms. Bridget Means and **Sage Design Studio** started helping us when Zuckerbook was produced on a laser printed and assembled with a stapler. She brought us out of the "obviously school made" realm into the world of the professional look, working with us to create a brand identity and dedicating her design studio to each issue of Zuckerbook twice per year at an unheard of discount. There is no way to thank her for her work other than to say that without her, we wouldn't be here.

Ms. Soshana Driver, **Ms. Kellie James King**, and **Ken and Eileen Babbs** have donated and sent us great pictures of Zuckerbook around the united States, from Seattle, Washington to Phoenix, Arizona, Dexter, oregon and beyond. It is wonderful to have great friends who love our work and love what we do enough to hand over some financial support and then super fun pictures of themselves enjoying Zuckerbook. Thank you, thank you, and thank you.

Ms. Sarah Callahan remains, and always shall remain, a spirit guide on our journey. Zuckerbook started, in part, because of her, and though she is taking time off from teaching to raise a family, she remains within the pages of this book. Bless her and the work that she does. She is a jewel in the crown of education and teaching.

And, to each of you, as always, thank you. This book is as much for you as the students and communty with which we work, and we remain grateful for your involvement. Thank you for deciding that Zuckerbook is worthy of support, thank you for purchasing our books and thank you for believing in our project. Without you, the energy to continue might not exist. We are grateful for your support, for you are the people who will spread the word, and will bring us into the front lines of young adult literature. Your support is valued beyond measure and drives our dedication to the process. It is, after all, the process, right?

The Mission of The Zuckerbook Project is, and shall remain, to produce the very highest quality student publication of literary works intermingled with visual art, while remaining faithful to the Zucker Middle School student experience, and then distribute it to the community, so that our voices may be heard. Let them always be heard.

Open it and read…

-- Mr. Frik J. Hilden, March 5th, 2022

Zuckerbook in Cambodia.   *photos by Gina Harris*

zuckerbook

Contents

Prologue

Since a prologue is, by nature, a way of introducing the book and letting the reader shake its hand, we thought we would write another one. There are always plenty of surprises.

How to introduce each chapter is, as you can well imagine, not so simple a task. But, because we are The Zuckerbook Project and insist on doing things our own way, here they are.

Critters that Skitter and Slither explores our students' connection to the animal kingdom. Sort of.

Angst be Angsty is all about that charming teenage attitude we all know and love - and how quick that can get out of control.

Ho Ho Horror digs into the holiday season with typical teenage sarcasm and views it as a horror show.

Edumacation is everything the typical Zucker Middle School student thinks about being in school. And learning. And homework. And everything.

Goose and Grimm continues our twice annual run of fairy tales as seen through the pubescent eye.

All Mixed Up goes spelunking into the caverns of teen-age confusion in the most heartwarming way, playing around with propaganda and other weird ideas.

Rhetoric Feels digs into what happens when honors students are turned loose with a fistful of rhetorical appeals and a wholebunch of feels. Fun!

Enjoy.

Erik J. Hilden
Faculty Advisor
The Zuckerbook Project

Janell Thomas

1 Critters that Skitter and Slither

Fish

Logan Bonilla

Fish come in different packages,
The ones that make people squeal in disgust,
The ones that are vibrant colors,
And portrayed in art,

And the ones that people fish to eat,
Fish are like us we come in different packages,
We believe in different things and
Abide by different laws,
We all do not look the same and
May not act the same,

But at the end of the day,
We will always be the same on the inside

The Cat With A Plan

Miguel Ramirez

As I try to pick up the cat who had
Fallen asleep on my bed.
It awakens and causes massive destruction.
"Oh no," I say to myself as the
Cat jumps from wall to wall,
Like a ninja in disguise.

N'Dea Greenwood

Little did I know he had a plan.
A very discrete plan.
I sit there, shocked, as the cat runs from

One side of the room To the other,
Back and forth he goes until eventually knocking over a cup
Full of water.

The cat jumps on my face as it gets scared half to death by its
Own plan.
I yell as I see the cat coming straight towards
Me like a speeding bullet.
I put my hands up ready for the impact and
Successfully caught it.
That is when I realized I messed up big time,
The cat has now peed all over me.

Animals

Learric Green

There are so many animals to meet out in the wild.
Even if some of them stomp on snakes or strike a sloth
From a tree.
Most animals are safe to be around, like cats,
They are basically weak lions.

Most animals are scared of us unless that animal
Is powered higher than a lion.
But other animals are nice and just hang out and
Do what they do.
Rabbits are similar to cotton balls, They are soft, fluffy,
And can get ripped up by other things.
But animals do what they do for survival,
They can be forgiven.

Unless they're a certain animal in the sea that launches other
Sea animals into the sky for fun.
In that case probably not gonna forgive them.
But I can forgive sloths.
Even if they aren't the smartest or fastest animal out there.

Even if they starve to death if leaves are on a plate and eat
Stuff that gives them no energy.

The Old Man And The Dog

Madisyn Tumbleston

The silent sound of the night gently creeps through,
The air as people walk past the cemetery by the
Old graves. The silent whisper of the departed fills
The air though people can not hear them and,

Summons for help to their loved ones.
Someone steps to the grave and puts
Down flowers and food so their loved ones
Can enjoy their last meal before daylight,

Hits the horizon. Daylight hits the graves
And now the voices are silent and the departed,
Fall into a long blanket of slumber as the hours
Goes past, waiting to see their families again.
The day goes past as people walk by
He homeless man who lives in a box on
5th avenue by himself.
He asks for food and water and money

As people ignore him and walk past,
To continue their daily activities.
One day a dog comes up to him wagging
His tail as he rolls over asking for food,
The man gives him a small portion of a
Frozen hotdog and pets him gently as he eats.
The old man left one day and forgot about the dog,

When he came back the dog had gathered up
Some food hoping that he will come back.
The old man runs to him crying and asking
For his forgiveness and all the dog could do
Was run up to him barking and wagging his tail.

The old man and the dog suddenly became
The best friend anyone has ever seen and
This is the poem that dog really is
Man's best friend.

Denisev Martinez

What Could That Be

Imani Wolfe-Macanic

Sometimes I wonder what that could be
Could it be an amazing wedding full of zebras,
Birds, tigers, lions of any sort or could it be a
A cow that mowed the garden while
Hanging out with bees and trees.

Or could it be humans and mermans
Hanging out with each other or could it be
The dog animals picking a fight like bees
Yelling at each other I guess we will never
Know during this weird, crazy, crazy day.

I thought I was right I guess I am wrong
It might just be my mind time-wasting
Thinking I hear those such things.

Christopher Lopez

As I Go To The Zoo

Malachi Pollard

As I go to the zoo
As I go to the zoo i see animals
As I go to the zoo i'll have fun
As I go to the zoo i'll be there for a while

As I go to the zoo i see wild cats
As i go to the zoo i see ocean animals
As i go to the zoo i see primary animals

As i go to the zoo i'll feed some of them
As i go to the zoo i'll pet some of them
As i go to the zoo i'll name them
As i go to the zoo i'll have to pay
And when i do it doesn't matter
Cause i have a good time

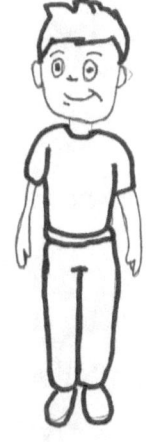

Brooke Cumbee

Rat Dig Holes

Malachi Pollard

A rat digs holes to find food,
A rat favorite food is cheese,
Or could it be its own kind.
This rat eats its own kind,

This rat is feared by its own kind.
This rat's favorite food is its own kind.
This rat has a plague like the black death.
But this Plague affect its own kind,
When a rat is bitten by this infected rat it turns faril.

This rat was made by hatred when he was
Experimented on,
When the rat escaped he hated the way he looked.
The rat was discriminated against by its own kind.
He hated them and ate them every single one,

The rat soon became big and muscular.
He ate ate every rat he seened,
He soon almost ate lab rats he saw.
He ate them all ate the rat became hungry he starved,
He became scrawny and frail then died.

Chloe Hwang

Olivia Sumerlin

2 Angst be Angsty

What I Hate

Gabrielle Myers

I hate when people talk when the
Classroom is supposed to be quiet.
I just hate when people are noisy and general.
ESPECIALLY when I'm focused.

I just hate when people break the silence.
I hate when people talk over me.
It's very annoying.
If I'm trying to talk to you, why are you talking over
Me?

I just hate when people won't let me finish.
I hate it when people ask me what I want to eat.
It's kind of like pressure.
When they ask me I can never think of anything.
I just hate when people ask me to make a choice.

The Anger Inside of Me

Iliana Domenech

The anger inside me.
I get mad when bad memories come back to my head,
Rethinking that I could have done better.
Loneliness dwells inside me and that makes me mad.
The anger inside.

I feel mad when I am reminded I have to cope with
My anxiety.

I am mad when people who don't have anxiety
Try to tell me to control,
When they don't know how hard it is.
It makes me mad.
The anger inside me.

The anger inside me.
Being sick makes me mad.
There is nothing to do when you are sick,
I know these things may not make you mad,
But they make Me mad.

Chloe Hwang

My Dear Rosa

Imani Wofe-Macanic

My dear Rosa, why did you leave?
There was something I was meaning to tell you,
Why did you leave me as if I'm just trash,
In the desert?

Oh dear rosa, have you heard the melodies
I make just for you?
Oh, you gotta hear them.
It is clear as the sky without a doubt,
You will forever be special to me.

My dear sweet rosa,
I thought you loved them.
I guess I was wrong.
Please come back and
Let me explain all of the things
I was trying to tell you,

Oh, dreams and nightmares
Scared as a deer near highlights.
Rosa please just listen to me,
Tell me about this nightmare.

Cara Dawn

My Brother

Miguel Ferguson

Always ticking me off my older brother.
As annoying as a mosquito,
He buzzes in my ears every minute,
Not knowing when to stop.

Even when studying he comes into my room,
Blasting the loudest music.
I've heard,
But because he is the oldest,

He doesn't even listen to me.

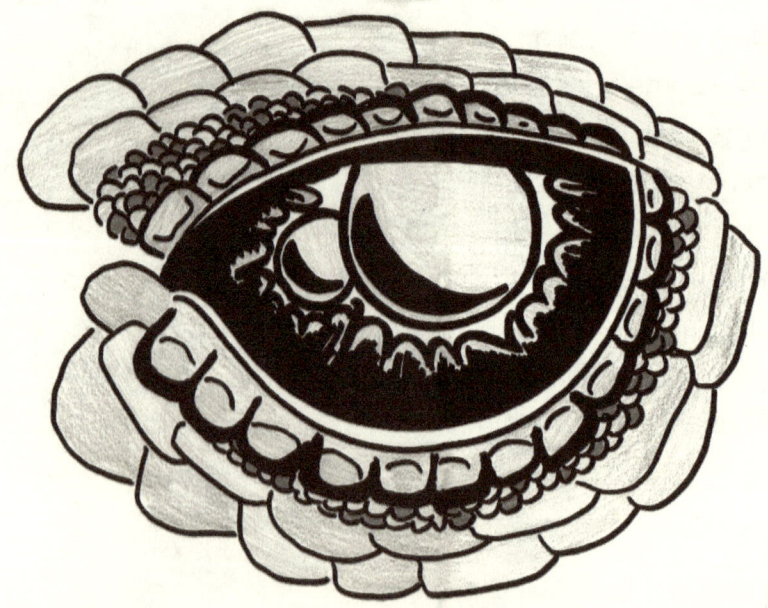

Jameson Perkins

Him

N'Dea Greenwood

His brown skin, his brown eyes,
The way he walks and talks.
He makes me feel safe; anybody that
Tries to play with me he steps in.
The sweetest but the most
A disrespectful person ever.
He makes me happy! He protects
I and you don't play with his idea now.his brown skin, his
Brown eyes make me
Get butterflies.
Everybody else gave me roach vibes.

He is everywhere. He won't leave me alone.
It's like walking around with a clone.
I just wanna go home. I told him to leave me alone.
He's obsessed; he got me stressed out

To the point, I can't take it anymore! He's not
Cool as a cucumber anymore. He's over barring
And pushing himself on me.
Leave Me alone and find somebody else.

But yet as I thought he was done he wasn't.
He asks who is that boy I hug;
He's my best friend why?
Jealousy. Disgusting.
Leave me alone yet I can't get away.

How Dare She?

Shyann Owens

How Dare She take my phone.
How dare She Step on my shoe.
How dare She insult my clothing.
How dare She think she's the best out of everyone.

How dare She hang out with MY friends.
How dare She try to get close to MY parents.
How dare She try to have a sleepover with me
As if we are best friends.
How dare She.

Ka'Naisha Green

Feelings vs. Attempt for Staying Heartless

Imani Wolfe-Macanic

What are these crazy things that hurt my heart
With waves of slowing beating just hit my heart?
What could it be, could it be feelings?

Oh if your feelings are okay?
Can you just explain why you got me
like this? I just want to feel heartless
Not an emotion or feelings?

May I please be free oh please
Just let me have the heartless self.
I thought you could stop.
I guess I am not right or wrong.

From now on this crazy mess going
Through my head whatever you're doing
To my brain, I root for change not to repeat
Things may you please just let go
Of my hand and just let me be from you.

Sussy

Gabrielle Myers

I think the word sussy is dumb.
It is the most DUMBEST word in the universe.
I hate when people use it.
I hate when people say it.

Who even came up with that word?
What would you even use it for?
"This plate is sussy"
See, it evens sounds dumb.

Sports Are Difficult

Vanessa Hunter

These two teenagers have a hard life.
They want to be together and also play sports,
The boy plays football and the girl plays volleyball.
It's hard because they're both busy all the time with their
life.

They're in love with each other too.
But one wants the other to quit their sport
and cheer them on in the bleachers,
While the other one wants both of them to
have an athletic life and still be together and in love.
But they hate that because they just want to be together.

Always together and live with each other,
But when they break up to enjoy their sports and do
good in life,
But they end up back together.
They start having problems with their relationship.

Most of the time they only talk in school,
And after that, there's no time for them to hang out
or talk to each other.
So during school out of nowhere,
they just stop talking to each other,
And ended the whole relationship.

The Choices Between Love and Hate

Brooklyn Nelson

The Choices Between Love and Hate
Why are love and hate such strong words?
It's sometimes hard to choose.
When you can't pick between the two.

The choices between love and hate
Sometimes you don't know who to love
Sometimes you don't know who to forgive
Even when they left you scarred

The choices between love and hate
The choices well leave weight on your shoulders
The choices well drain you
The choices well having slowly

The choices between love and hate
The choices be

Brooke Cumbee

You Brought Me Alive from the Dark

Oliva Reyes

You brought me peace and love
You brought a light to my darkness
Even when I thought I will be alone in
The dark, Even when I thought I could

Have never loved you the way I do
When all I had for you was hate and
Revenge to make you pay for what you did
But one by one you made me see who you

Really was, What you actually felt and how
Much you cared for me. It might not
Be the perfect and loving story out there
But I do know that it is OUR love story.

Daniel Jenkins

Real Nerd

Mely Flores

Why must everything be so difficult?
Why am I proven smart?
Why are people always being compared to me?
Why am I the leader and you are the followers?

Why have I continued to do what I have to do?
Why is this even the way to do things?
Why this much work?
Why am I still trying to prove something
That I can't even reach?

This is so hard, can I drop out?
They said no, that I must continue to fight.
I wanna know how the other class is doing.
Although my expectations are high.

I am still not able to reach them myself.
Always asking why but never asking how.
I wanna go to a good high school to make my mother proud,
There is a brick wall ahead of me though.

I Once Loved You But Now It's Hate

Iliana Domenech

I once loved you but now it's hate.
That day I saw you with my best friend instead of me,
My heart shattered into a million pieces.
Once loved but now its hate

I walk the halls with no one to hold onto instead you hold on to
My best friend.
I struggle to look you in the eyes without crying.
You let swim down to the darkness.
Once loved but now its hate

I once loved you but now it's hate.
You let sink into my sorrow,
This is a heartbreak I will never forget.
Once loved but now its hate

Now I walk the halls with my head high.

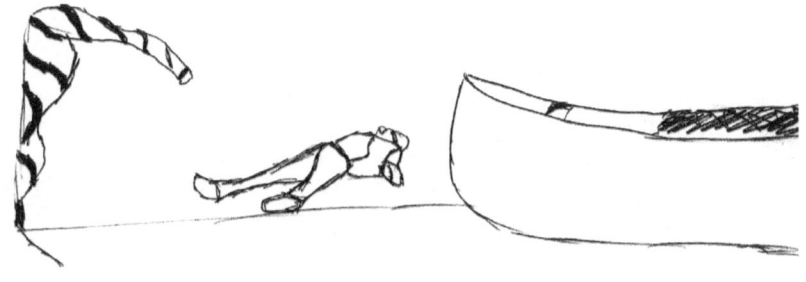

My Cousins Love

Miguel Ferguson

My cousin had been carried away by love until,
One Day something happened.
His girlfriend randomly called and said she liked someone else,
He was broken.

I've never seen him so broken.
As fast as lightning he ended up,
Getting over it.
His ex-girlfriend was surprised

He had gotten another girlfriend.
That made her jealous,
Even though she was the one,
That broke up with him.

He had forgotten that,
Day and would not speak to her.
After what she has done.

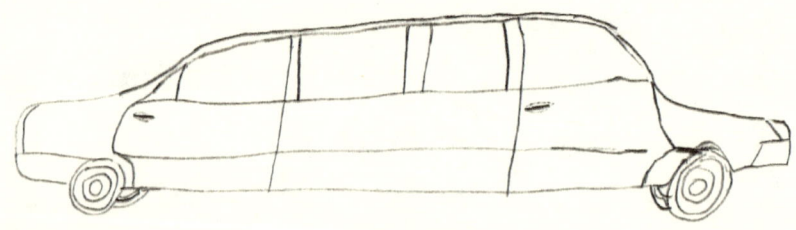

Brooke Cumbee

What Is love?

Micayah Seabrook

What is love?
I find myself asking that. I wonder if love is
Something that can unbreak the broken.
Unhurt the hurt. Unshed these shedding tears.
Hear the unspoken. See the unseen.

Is it something that
Will hold me close when
I have dreams of my wretched past?
Will it soothe me and tell me
It's going to be alright?

Will it judge me when I tell it
What I have been through ,or will it say
That there is nothing wrong with you?
When I'm cold at night, will it hug me
With its warmth? When I need it will it be
Just like when I need my father?

Is love even all that great that people
Make it out to be? I don't think that I will
Ever know
Until I
Experience
It.

Oliva Sumerlin

3 Ho Ho Horror

Christmas Fear

By Breózinay Saulsberry

Two days before Christmas I was feeling numb,
And having nightmares day after day.
At night my friend visited me,
And I was home and I was laying down.
But a new day cameand nightmares continued.
Barely walking, couldn't feel anything, crying.
My body was wasted. I called the ambulance,
And I ended up in the hospital at night.

The Nightmare on Christmas

By Oliver Sosa

It was a dark stormy night all the kids were in fright
A night before Christmas not a nightmare in sight
I had finally gone to bed and
When I woke up everyone was dead.
Blood all over the walls all you can see was red

It was the Nightmare on Christmas on top of the roof
I told all my friends and they called me a goof
They said he's not real do you have any proof
I showed them the room everything was gone
The room was so empty it looked like I was wrong
It felt like a nightmare but so realistic
Maybe it was real or maybe it was fake
Maybe going to sleep was a mistake.

I was trapped in a dream where everyone was dead
A room full of blood and rotting heads
I met the nightmare and the one thing he said
In order to escape this dream,
you have to slice your own head

I decided and it took quite a while
The nightmare grinning like a crocodile

Heads on Christmas Day

By Arson Clayton

On Christmas day
With smiles on our faces
We open our presents

We look in to see
Smiles still on our faces
The heads of our parents

We stare in shock
As we go on to the next
The biggest presents we have

We unwrap it
And open it to see
The heads of our parents' parents

Are you on the naughty list?
Do you run around and not listen to your parents
Well maybe you too
Would like to open a present
That holds the heads of your parents.

Ka'Naisha Green

DAD?

By Ryan Chaplin

Santa Claus comes once every year,
Santa brings the Christmas cheer!
Going through chimneys,
I ask him for a kidney for my cat,
Timmy who's passing away,
I've never seen his face.
Santa always runs away,
No one questions this, why won't he stay?

I set a trap for him on Christmas day.
Mom called me from the kitchen.
She told me to listen,
As she sharpens utensils for her turkey, that's plain.

"Santa sleigh got stuck in the rain therefore,
He will be delayed."
"That's great mom," I say,
More time for me to play.
I try to stay sane.

Thinking about the pain Santa could obtain,
Oh no, I'm not insane.
His pain will not be in vain,
It's for Timmy, my cute sick kitty.

Also, dad is coming to the city,
8:00 hits, It's my dad that I miss.
He's always out doing business
He gives me moments of bliss.

I know he won't miss this Christmas,
I went to take a nap.
I forgot about Santa and the trap,
I go downstairs and hear a loud tap.

It must be Santa that collapsed,
I found my catch!
Santa squirms like a worm,
I went to get the utensils that were more than warm,

I lunge the utensils in his side that contained my prize,
For my little sick kitty Timmy.
I went curious while the hurt Santa grew furious,
I moved his beard then looked into his face.

Mely Flores

The Morning of Christmas

By Brooke Cumbee

The family of 7 descend the stairs,
Tumbling and pushing until they arrive at the tree
Presents shimmering and neatly wrapped lay below the tree.
Not knowing what awaits inside these neatly wrapped boxes.

The children waited for their father for hours
Until their mother caved.
Each picking our presents,
They started to unwrap their biggest present first,
The mother sitting in the chair recording.

A scream echoed from the oldest child
When opened the biggest and shiniest present of all,
The box seeping from the fathers bloodied head.
None of them noticed the man grinning
From the window while watching everything.

Jose Aguilar

The Massacre

By Brooke Cumbee

Their guts and limbs lay
Axes and sharp chainsaws swing
The families being torn apart
They were chopped down till there were no more

They lay limp sitting until the people return
When they return they wrap
Them so they don't fall apart more
Slung around then thrown into trucks
Piled on top of each other and stacked

Their dead bodies are sold to families
Who stands them back up like their alive
Strings bright lights and shiny ornaments
On their limbs and branches
Naming the bodies…

Christmas Trees

Brooke Cumbee

The Nightmare

By Nathen Jones

The night of joy and fun
And someone stole your son
Nuts and bolts filled the room with a clatter
And down fell a ladder

When you went downstairs
You found some odd stares
But ignoring it and back up the stairs you went
And realized you were hell-bent

Back to sleep, you go
While watching 8 Mile with your bros
The next day you awoke
And the house started to smoke

Denisev Martinez

And when you saw the fire
You realize that you have a lighter
Down the house when with ash
You stared while scratching your rash.

When you filed your statement
You looked up and saw the pennant
After you left the county
You left behind your bounty

You awoke from your nightmare
And you pet your dog named Bear
You went downstairs with your family to open gifts
After you made your last wish

During your dreams, you heard Stan
At the concert with Eminem's fans.

Ulises Oliva

Santa and the Deaths on Hopeless Street

Trawley Harper

Deaths deaths struck once again
On hopeless lane on christmas night.
Nothing but deaths is all you had seen
What should you do? Should you find
Out who did this such thing?

During this christmas night if there is
No one but you, almost everyone on
Your street is dead but you, of course,
But you gotta find out what's truly going on.

Cause there are so many dead bodies
Murdered you gotta find a way to find this killer.
Hold on! You saw Santa with a chainsaw!
He might be the killer, so beware

Chanel Drayton

And watch your back we got a killer
Lurking around, and I meant what I said!
Really! Watch carefully where you go.
No one is safe.

Do not make a sound, not even a peep,
Just stay silent and you will be safe.
You really thought you will live. You guessed
Wrong, cause he was near. You can't run away,

Cannot even fight this. it's time for you
To die, like you never ever existed.
But this is his lane now so step away!
Cause he came with a Bang! Boom! Pow!

Denisev Martinez

Janell Thomas

4 Edumacation

Just Be Yourself

Victoria Flores

That's not cool,
Flexing your good grades isn't cool.
Hanging with the popular kids isn't cool.
Getting an app everyone has isn't cool.

It's just not cool.
Maybe you want attention,
But that's not a good way.
Just be yourself,

And don't copy what others say.

Where's My Phone?

Sarah Finkley

Ahhhh! I ran out of my bed and washed my face.
I dashed to my room and put my clothes on along with my,
Socks and shoes, oh no there's not a lot of time for breakfast.
So I hurried along and got my bookbag.
I went and said goodbye.

To Mama but she was sound asleep
So if I'm late that's my problem.
I grabbed my key and walked out the door and,
The bus was already down the street.
The kids had already got on the bus so I ran faster.

And faster saying "Please don't leave me!"
The bus took off in a blink of an eye I stopped.
To get my phone but realized I left it at home.
So I ran back to the house. And there I quietly
Walked back and looked all around. Under the couch,

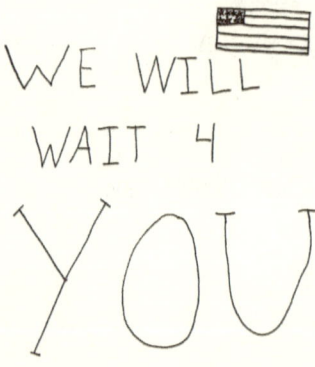

WE WILL
WAIT 4
YOU

Mely Flores

In the dirty clothes, in the kitchen, and in Mama's room.
Then I thought I left it on my bed so I tossed
The covers and it hit my head. I turned it on and it's
7:30, and my school starts at 7:40.
I refuse to wake mama up once more because

I will get a serious punishment.
So I built up the courage and decided that
I will walk to school.
I went out the front door and walked
farther and farther away.

Saw my bus and kid with their head out the window.
The bus was picking up kids,
And I ran towards the bus.
I turned my phone on and it was 7:37. "Yes!"

I screamed because I dodged a punishment
And was late for school again.

Cara Dawn

School

Brooke Cumbee

I hate school.
School sucks for many reasons,
8 hours of boredom,
Teachers who make sure you are not on your phone.

I hate school.
That one student who knows every bad word,
When that one student's name literally means angel,
When he is the absolute opposite.

I hate school.
When your locker lock just stops working.
When you get in trouble for something you didn't do,
When you really want to go home but can't,

I hate school.

Ka'Naisha Green

Work You Have To Do

Isabella Villegas

There's work you have to do,
But you really don't do anything.
Basically, you just spent your time procrastinating.
You really hate homework,
A little bit too much,
But one in specific
Will make you work all night
And make you wanna cry.

Tick-tock, the time is passing by,
You haven't done almost anything
So you have to improvise.
Try to remember everything in class,
Even though you didn't understand.
It felt like an eternity,
But finally, you ended up finishing it all.

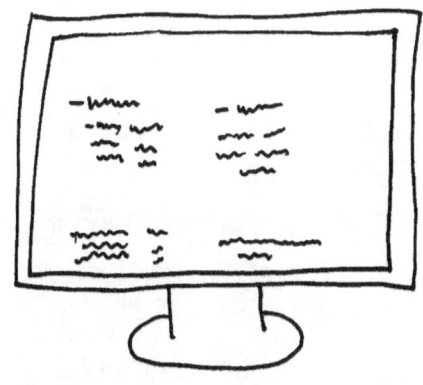

Mely Flores

Oh, God!

Taymar Alston

Oh, God!
Referrals, conferences, write-ups,
I can't seem to get it right! Can't get my way
Because I act stubborn, they say but I don't
Believe them, I blame it on them and pay the
Consequences but still don't seem to understand.
Oh, God!
I can't seem to get it right! They still say
That I'm judging
Them and they're trying to
Look out for me, but I don't believe them.
They claim that I know and just
Don't wanna listen, but that's not it!
Oh, God!
I just can't seem to get it right!
I'm starting to understand and fix my problem,
But they don't believe me because I lied too much in
The past, they still don't understand, I'm trying to fix
My problem!
Oh, God!
I finally fix my problem, but still have of days,
I try my best to keep it straight but I
Keep getting distracted, I don't understand the
The problem, is I'm too nervous to ask for help,
I'm like a monkey
When a human is trying to teach it English!
Oh, God!

Laughter, Sadness, and Joy

Taymar Alston

School brings me laughter, sadness, and joy.
I learn something new every day and make good grades.
It's mostly cold but the warmth of having
A good royal friend brings me joy!
School brings me laughter, sadness, and joy.

School brings me laughter and joy when
We have events like field trips, assemblies,
And hanging with my friends.
School brings me laughter, sadness, and joy.
I am filled with joy when I am recognized.
It brings me joy to see and hear others
Do very good things and feel good about it.

School brings sadness when I see others in trouble.
Sadness is such a strong word that makes people hurt.
It is sad when sadness gets a hold of your mind because
People can do many crazy things.
School brings me laughter, sadness, and joy.

School is such a great place where everyone stays safe.
School is the best place to be when you don't feel
As happy as you can be.
School is almost like home but I have many more friends
And learn about many things.

School brings me laughter, sadness, and joy.

Olivia Sumerlin

5 Goose and Grimm

The Big Adventure

by Cole Palzer

Once upon a time, in a shadowy forest, inside a castle, which was a large semi-broken down castle. Three people named Crescent, Robin, and Blaze were sitting at a table near the throne room. They have been explaining to each other about the Battle of The Devour; they would always talk about how their ancestors lost that battle, and how someday they will defeat Samael. The two knights of the castle would always listen to the three of them talking about that. The knights would always wonder why they couldn't just talk about something else.

Chef Marissa then invited Crescent, Robin, and Blaze for dinner, including the two knights and the rest of the 200 people that were inside the castle. Once everyone sat at the huge dining table, everyone picked out the food they wanted, and the feast began. Of course, Crescent, Robin, and Blaze were picky eaters, they didn't eat much and only had sweet things like candy and stuff.

"Oh my sweet babies," said Marissa ,"you guys have to eat something healthy unless you wanna starve."

Although Crescent and Robin were tempted by Marissa's voice, they ignored her and went outside in the vast space of the dark forest. In the forest, all three of them sat on a branch of a tree and started chatting. Blaze noticed that there was some type of red sphere-forming in the sky, and started to tell both Crescent and Robin to look up. They told Blaze it's nothing to worry about, and that it happens all the time in the middle of the night. Blaze saw that the red sphere started to get bigger, and then BOOM... It created a loud noise, Blaze screamed, "WATCH OUT BRO! IT'S HEADING TOWARD US!!!"

Everyone and Robin looked at each other and then looked back at what seemed like large hands coming towards them. The hands had large sharp claws and teared-up skin. They all looked at each other wondering why those hands were coming towards them. They were thinking so much ahead that they didn't notice it was meters away from them, then the large hands wrapped around them and pulled them into the red sphere. Later that day, most of the people in the castle noticed that Crescent, Robin, and Blaze were gone, Marissa and the two knights decided to put up "Missing Person" posters for all three of the kids. They waited days and days worrying what could have happened to them, most of the people suspected that they got snatched by raiders, some other people thought they had just run away somewhere in the distance of the forest. In the dark void which was very dark and damp with torches as the only source of light, stood Crescent, Robin, and Blaze, they were confused and worried about what happened. They were trying to figure out where they were or what they were in.

Blaze questioned Crescent and Robin, saying, "What just happened??" Each of them was confused and decided to walk and find someone to guide them. As they were walking they noticed lots of hooded figures off in the distance, they decided not to bother since they didn't want any trouble. Then one of the hooded figures came up to them and asked what they needed help with. Robin said that he and his friends needed to know where they were and how to get out of here. The hooded figure greeted them and asked to follow them, Crescent asked "Where are you taking us?" The hooded figure replied and said, "I am taking you to the courtroom."

Ka'Naisha Green

As they were walking to the courtroom the hooded figure told the three of them that his name was Abaddon and that he was going to ask certain stuff about why they were here. Crescent remembered at the last second that they were snatched away by those hands and told Abaddon what happened and why they got here. Abaddon gave a slight grudge and continued walking. A couple of minutes later they got towards a large door, and Abaddon then got out a special spellbook and did a little spell on the door to open it. Once the doors opened, it revealed a large room, with chains hanging from the ceiling, large pillars with weird symbols on them, and what looked like a ritualistic stage. Abaddon told the 3 of them to step on the stage and wait for others to come.

Micayah Seabrook

Blaze said, "Where are we?" Crescent told Blaze that they are probably going to be held in some type of court trial since Abaddon is suspicious about them being here.

After a long wait, Abaddon and a bunch of other people came in and sat on big chairs near Crescent, Robin, and Blaze. Abaddon then took off his hood to reveal a decrepit head with 4 large horns and 6 eyes.

All 3 of them looked worried and thought they were about to get eaten or something like that. Robin then asked, "What are you going to do to us?" Abaddon then dashed towards Robin and told Robin to stay quiet. Robin looked at Abaddon with an angry look, but then let it go and decided to deal with what was going to happen to them. A long time later a large entity came into the room, it had a large dragon-like skull with 2 large curved horns, and what seemed like its body was made from gemstones, it also had 4 arms with razor-sharp claws. In a deep voice, the entity said,

"Welcome humans, I am Samael, and I and my fellow guardians will ask you some questions." Crescent, Robin, and Blaze were surprised about what the Devour said, they expected to be killed or tortured, but they were only going to be asked questions, what a relief they wondered.

Samael then explained everything else, and then went on with the questions. Everyone in the room asked the 3 of them questions, like, "How did you get in our world," or "Are you guys, intruders?"

After what seemed like an eternity of questioning,

Samael asked the last question which was "Where are you people from?"

Blaze answered, "We are from the castle, Saint Evernore."

Samael looked surprised from what they had just said, Samael then explained that he and the people at Saint Evernore had a conflict with each other and how back then they always had wars and chaos. Abaddon then cut in and restated the question asking "How did you guys get in our world?" Crescent replied and said that they were sucked/grabbed my hands from a weird red sphere thing, and then they ended up here.

"So that's why our high commandment guards didn't come back, YOU GUYS ACCIDENTLY WENT THROUGH OUR PORTAL EVEN THOUGH IT WAS MEANT FOR OUR GUARDS!" screamed Abaddon.

Denisev Martinez

Then 3 hooded figures came to each Crescent, Robin, and Blaze, and dragged them to a smaller door in the courtroom. After all the After alleged inside through the door into a room that seemed like some type of prison. All 3 of them asked what was going on and why they were going in here, but the 3 guards ignored them and threw them down onto the spikey floor.

After a couple of seconds, fleshy-mouth things that were connected to the wall opened up and grabbed each one of them inside with flesh-like appendages. Then all of them were chained up from their arms to their legs, they were now stuck inside the prison where they couldn't get out... Maybe they should have never gone outside during nighttime and should have listened to their fellow people who warned them, the 3 of them cried for help but no one came.

I guess now all of them were trapped in there for all eternity, or maybe until they got released somehow, they didn't understand what was going on. They didn't mean to do anything wrong but I guess the moral of the story is to never do something out of your free will when there could be consequences for your actions...

A couple of days later, Crescent, Robin, and Blaze were still stuck inside the prison. They've been calling for help ever since but no one came, they all thought that they would just die in the disgusting place with no food or water. Though they have been hearing a lot of loud noise throughout the days and wondered if it was the fighting and clashing of the people trying to save them, they did doubt that since no one would have the common sense to know where they were. A couple of seconds later all 3 of them heard someone come into the prison room and then there was a loud BANG. Bright light filled the room and Crescent, Robin and Blaze noticed that the flesh mouths were blown open and there was a large figure of dark obsidian-like armor with lava streaks running down it.

The large figure told the 3 of them to come with him, and that he will save them from this place. Robin asked "Who are you?"

The large figure replied, saying, "You'll see once I get you back to safety." As they were running and trying to get out of this place, Crescent, Robin, and Blaze noticed that there were lots of hooded people that seemed to be dead or at least hurt enough to not be conscious anymore. Crescent wondered to herself if the large armored guy did this, so she decided not to ask since she was more worried about getting home safely.

All four of them took various routes throughout the area, going from one place to another trying to find an exit. After what felt like a couple of hours they finally came back to the area where they first came from, well at least where Crescent, Robin, and Blaze came from.

As the hooded figure was making some type of portal Samael then came and tried to grab Crescent, Robin, and Blaze but then the large armored person protected them and was the one who got caught. The armored figure then yelled at the 3 of them and told them to go into the portal, they hesitated.

Why would they just let someone who helped them get snatched away by some ugly God?

They decided to step it anyways, once they stepped in, their vision was blinded for a couple of seconds, and then they were falling from the sky they then landed on the ground softly somehow without getting hurt.

Needless to say, they were all fine, they were not suffering from any cuts or bruises or any damage from being trapped in a prison for days. They lived happily ever after…

Olivia Summerlin

The Real Evil

By Ryan Chaplin

Long ago in a small magical town, there was a community filled with magic and magical clothing. Once an article of clothing was purchased, it could not be sent back or returned. In the small magical town, there was a small family of a girl and her two parents. She was named Yolo because her parents believed that you should live life to the fullest. Afterall, you only live once.

"Mom! What time do we go shopping?" Asked Yolo.

"After, we have to watch the town news," the mother explained. Moments later, the town news began.

"Greetings everyone, here is today's news," the news reporter began.

Vicky Flores

"This is a time that children go to get their magical clothing, there are many colors to choose from in this period! Parents, do you recall MTC? It's been noted that they are back at it again, so avoid buying your children red and black clothing. That is all the news for today, Have a great one!" The reporter then ended the news.

"Who is MTC?" Yolo asked her parents.

"They are a vicious gang that enjoys eradicating this town. They have been doing so for centuries. You should be aware of anyone wearing black or red," Yolo's dad explained.

"Why can I not wear red? Because of those evils? Why when people wearing those pastel colors commit a crime they don't get their color canceled?" Yolo said in an annoyed tone.

"It's not really for us to know, Yolo. We only obey the town's rules, Let's go shopping!" Yolo's mom said to her.

Yolo shrugged it off while being annoyed by the town's news and her parents. Moments later they are at the magical town shop which is very popular for getting magic and magical clothing. They walked into the half-empty shop which was packed. As clothing disappeared more appeared. Then a dress caught Yolo's eye, A lonely red dress on a shelf. The shelf had a sign that said "forbidden" in large red font. The red dress sat on the shelf lonely, the red dress complained about their dreadful life being on the shelf.

"This stupid town, why couldn't my creator allow one of my magics to be disappearing?" The red dress whined.

"Oh wow, mom look! There is an ugly evil dress in the shop," One of the bratty customers muttered.

"Oh my! Let's leave before something bad happens."

The mom then hurried her and her kid out of the store.

The "forbidden" dress has gone through this ever since it was created. It all started when one of the most famous royals was bored...

"Hans! Come here!" The royalty yelled.

"I am bored again, is there anything fun and trendy to do these days?" The royalty asked Hans who is a servant.

"You can make a magical dress ma'am," Hans told the royalty.

"Ugh! Do not call me ma'am! It makes me feel old!" The royalty scolded Hans.

"Is it legal for me to do that? I'm not certified," The royalty questioned Hans.

"Well, you can make one for fun. I will get the equipment!" Hans told the royalty while scurrying out the room.

He then brought out the equipment with a vast and dusty magic book. He then sat the text on the table.

"Oh geez! That thing must be older than my ancestors," The royalty exclaimed while coughing from the book dust.

She viewed the equipment and saw that her options for colors were limited to red and pink. The royalty was a naturally born troll so she chose red to frighten Hans because she knew he heard and was scared about the news. She finished the dress in less than 5 hours and Hans noticed that.

"Voila! Now let's sell it" the royalty beamed looking forward to seeing Hans' frightened expression.

"What! Do you not see the color of that!?" Hans questioned her in fear.

"Why? Is it too dangerous for you?" The royalty taunted Hans.

"Well, what type of positive did you apply to it? Maybe that will break the curse of that color," Han asked.

Olivia Summerlin

"Who said I wanted to break the 'curse'?" The royalty snickered. Now Yolo adores the dress the royalty effortlessly made.

"Mom and Dad, I know it is supposed to be forbidden but that dress is so cute!" Yolo exclaimed loudly. She got a few stares in return.

"Is she one of the psychopaths ruining this town?" One of the customers silently questioned Yolo rudely.

"It's in the forbidden section for a reason, Yolo," Her dad hissed.

"Okay, dad, I see that but it is still in the store for a reason. Right, Mom?" Yolo replied.

"Your dad is right. It's not on an open shelf for a reason and you do not want to look like an MTC member," Yolo's mom explained.

Yolo scoffed at her parents. Yolo wanted to prove the town wrong about this worry, but then she began to question herself.

Jameson Perkins

"What if all this panic is for good?" Yolo silently questioned herself. She shrugged her thoughts off and sneaked towards the dress.

Yolo admired the dress quietly and touched every piece of the dress hems and designs. She wondered how this beautiful mess of art is deemed so dangerous.

"Ugh! Get your grubby hands off of me!" The red dress snapped.

"Woah! You speak?" Yolo quaked.

In this magical town, it was normal for things like insects and animals to talk but never inanimate objects. Yolo began shaking in her boots while the red dress looked at her in disgust.

"Aren't I speaking right now? What do you want? If you want to insult me then go ahead. There is nothing you will say that I have not heard before."

The red dress hissed, without thinking Yolo hurried and shoved the dress in her bag which caused an employee to look at her in suspicion. The employee noticed that the red dress was suddenly gone. Yolo tried to run off without looking suspicious but the manager stopped her in her tracks.

"Hey! Have you seen that red dress? It was here before you came," The employee questioned her.

"Um...Uh... no I have not seen a red dress," Yolo answered nervously.

A manager noticed and went towards them.

"What is wrong? Why are you questioning this child?" The manager asked.

"The forbidden dress somehow disappeared when

she appeared," the employee rudely explained. The manager sighed.

"At least that evil thing is out of here," the manager whispered to the employee but loud enough that Yolo still heard him.

"Go ahead and run along little girl. Have a nice day," the employee said with a sarcastic tone. Yolo went to locate her parents while the red dress was still in her backpack.

"I think we should go home because I cannot find a dress and I want to do some research before I buy one," Yolo quickly lied to get her parents to leave the store.

"Um, I guess we could go but you need a dress before Monday," Yolo's mom explained.

"Okay mom, now let's go now!" Yolo said as she hurried out of the shop. Yolo then came home. She went straight to her room to inspect the dress.

"Before you say anything, how do you talk?" Said Yolo. After she said that a big swoosh of wind went around the room and the dress began to float.

"I talk with my magic," the red dress explained.

"So is it true that you curse people who wear you?" Yolo asked.

"Put me on then we will see," The red dress snickered.

The night passed slowly and was full of panic because once Yolo had put the dress on, It would not come off! She ended up falling asleep with the dress on so she could confront her parents about it.

"Oh my, Yolo where did you get that dress?" Yolo's

parents yelled at her in fear.

"I got it from the shop yesterday and now I can not take it off," Yolo cried.

"We thought you said you could not find a dress," the mom questioned Yolo.

"I lied mom, now how will I take this off? I have to go to school today," Yolo cried.

"I am sorry, Yolo, but it is a rule that once you put on your magical clothing, you cannot take it off." Yolo had to go to school in a red dress, and as expected, she was stared at a lot.

Olivia Summerlin

"Why would they let a criminal in the school? Did everyone forget about the news?" one of the students said. The principal then called Yolo because people kept reporting seeing that she had on a red dress and thought she was a part of MTC.

"Yolo, please come to the front office," the principal demanded Yolo. Yolo arrived at the front office and there were many officers there.

"Let's get straight to the point. Have you not heard the news lately? We will not accept evil in this school!" The principal shouted at Yolo then all of a sudden the school began shaking like there was an earthquake. As the room was shaking Yolo rose into the air with dark red eyes as if something was summoning her.

"I told you guys she was a criminal!" A student shouted while they watched the demonic-like scene take place. Jets began to land on the school property and well-known villains started to make their way towards Yolo.

"We have not had one of these happen since decades ago! Our arch-nemeses has come back for some reason! How will we defeat them!?" A school staff yelled.

The arch-nemeses made their way to Yolo but they stopped as they saw more jets come. Many people were a part of MTC who were coming out of the jets.

"It looks like they are teaming up to destroy this town!" A civilian yelled.

"It's not like that at all!" An MTC member yelled at the civilian.

"Can you guys stop screaming and fight?!" The royalty that suddenly appeared yelled.

"MTC fight!" one of the MTC members yelled. Every-one in the MTC began to attack the arch-nemeses. Yolo even joined to help them because her magic formed while she was in the air. After the long and brutal war. The MTC group defeated the nemeses.

"I wish we never doubted them and the magic that they hold," one of the civilians cried. After they defeated the town's nemesis, many of the civilians began to honor them. Some of the citizens even apologize to MTC for the accu-sations. Days have passed since the war happened. There was a town meeting hosted by the young royalty.

"Hello, humans, fairies, elves, and our other magical creatures of this town. I have a crucial message. I will be giving my royalty spot up for someone special. Yolo! She is the youngest person to ever fight our arch-nemeses. Not only that, but she is also wearing my creations. Yolo, please come up and speak your peace, new royalty." The ex-royal-ty said while bowing to Yolo.

"They were never evil. They were gifted protectors of this town. They were not the people committing these crimes. Their image was sabotaged. Even though there were not many crimes committed, you all still ensured they were treated as if they destroyed this town. Now you guys honor them as your heroes. You guys separating this town was the real evil."

Yolo said then sashayed away in the beautiful red dress.

Olivia Summerlin

The Candy City Tragedy

Sanai' Branton

Once upon a time, there was a delightful little girl who lived in the Candy Kingdom, in a small candy cottage, and her name was Candypop. She was very kind-hearted and hated disobedience. Candypop always listened to her parents and followed all the rules, But her sister Lollipop was the complete opposite. Lollipop loved adventure, But she also did everything her parents told her not to do.

Mom said, "Walk." She ran.

Dad said, "Talk." She screamed.

The family lived in a big, colorful, beautiful candy kingdom. The sky was a berry-blue, the grass was gummy apple green, the people were friendly, and the clouds were as fluffy as cotton candy. The kingdom was as peaceful as could be. Then there was Grimsland. In Grimsland there lived vicious Gremlins who were hurting the kingdom. They were destroying palaces, eating candy cottages, and even throwing trash in the wells. Once before there was a food shortage in the kingdom because Gremlins were invading and taking their food supplies. Candypop and Lollipop could only go outside to play sometimes. Their parents were afraid that something bad could have happened to them. All the other families were leaving left to right.

Candypop and Lollipop's family was the only family that still lived in that kingdom for a while. Their parents decided that they'd move somewhere else for a better living environment. They moved to a bigger, better, and sweeter kingdom named CandyTopia. The kingdom had twice the candy cottages than the last. There were way more kids there, so Candypop and Lollipop could make new friends. Fast forward they have been living in Candy Topia for a week. Everything was going well, they had no worries, and their new life was wonderful, But then the Gremlins relocated to Grimsland. Just right across from Candy Topia. Unfortunately for the Gremlins, they couldn't get in Candy Topia as long as the gate was closed. Fortunately for the candy people, they had everything they needed in their kingdom.

Every time they left to play, their mother always shouted, "Don't go out of the gate! It is risky and dangerous!"

Well of course Candypop followed the rules, but Lollipop wanted to test that theory.

On a really hot day, Lollipop decided that the pool would be fun. She suggested her idea to Candypop and she thought it would be fun as well. They went and told their parents where they were going to the pool. Their parents wondered where the pool was but trusted them enough to let them go anyway. After their parents agreed to let them go, they were on their way.

As they were walking. They came to a stop. They ended up stopping at the kingdom gates. Candypop was confused about why they were there and Lollipop was nervous to tell her why they were there. Lollipop wanted to go so bad, that she forgot to tell Candypop where the pool was.

Lollipop explained, "You and I want to go to the pool, right?"

Candypop replied, "Yes"

Lollipop then continued, "The problem is the pool is outside of Grimland. If we go fast to the pool and run back, we should be back in no time."

Candypop was so angry she shouted, "Are you dumb!? You want to do what mom said not to do in the first place?!" Candypop got her towel, turned around, and started walking home until Lollipop grabbed her towel and tried to convince her not to go. Lollipop knew what Candypop hated the most, and that was being challenged.

So Lollipop then said, "Candypop, are you scared? If you aren't up for the challenge I understand." Candypop turned around quickly, looked Lollipop in the eyes, and said, "I'm not afraid of anything."

Lollipop said, "Prove it."

Candypop had so much regret and didn't know what to do. She didn't want to disobey her mother but couldn't turn down a challenge. Candypop just couldn't swallow her pride and she went along with Lollipop's plan. They turned around and walked back to the gate, before having to dash past Grimsland. Candypop still was having second thoughts about going.

But she couldn't let Lollipop think that she was scared. Meanwhile, Lollipop was ready and counted down.

"1! 2! 3!" The two of them shouted.

The two went speeding past Grimsland.

They thought nobody would've seen them running, but they thought wrong. A vicious, dirty, rough-skinned, gremlin named Gutter Guss happened to be walking along his way. He would've been more than pleased to capture one candy person and make them a meal, But two? In his eyes, It was a feast. Guss saw Lollipop and Candypop before they saw him. When he did, he made a signal to the other gremlins that there was food. Candypop saw all the gremlins and Guss rushing towards them.

Candypop saw them and immediately screamed, "Runnn!"

As soon as Lollipop saw, she headed straight for the kingdom gates.

They were both trying to escape being captured. They were quickly running out of time and the gremlins were getting closer to them. Every inch they ran, Candy Topia's gates seemed farther and farther. Lollipop ended up getting away. Two groups of Gremlins each running in the directions as the girls. The gremlins thought that they would have caught a meal. Unfortunately, they were too slow to catch both of them.

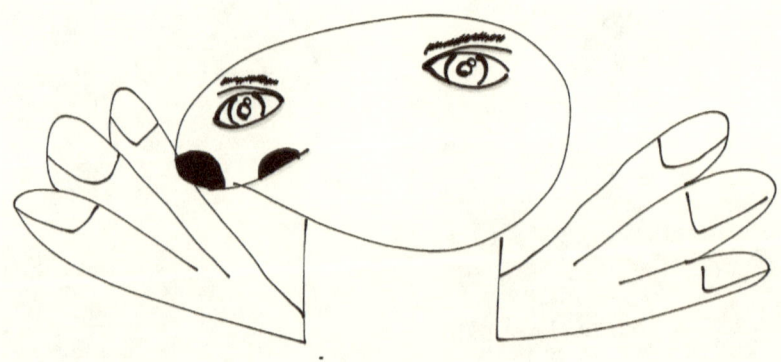

In relief, Lollipop was at the Candy Topia gates and thought that Candypop was right behind her. She was typing in the code to open the gate. Lollipop was trying to get in fast and close the gate before anyone saw it was opened.

While she walked into the kingdom, she speculated that Candypop was right behind her. She was laughing as if it was just a little incident that just happened. She didn't hear Candypop, finally turned around, and saw Candypop wasn't there. Lollipop went into a panic. She felt guilty because her Candypop didn't want to go in the first place and she pressured her into going. Now knowing she left her sister, she ran back as fast as she could to look for her. She unlocked the gate and ran out of the kingdom. But the Gremlins were nowhere to be found.

Lollipop kept running around looking for Candypop. It was very scary because any Gremlin could have seen and captured Lollipop as well, But she had no time for fear. The one thing she worried about was finding her sister. Lollipop ran and ran until she ended up in front of Grimsland. She had to take a deep breath and went inside. The gate to Grimsland was cracked open, so she was able to sneak in. When Lollipop got a closer look she noticed Gremlins assembling, crowning around something. When she peeked from behind a building, she was able to get a better view of the Gremlins assembly. Lollipop saw Candypop in a cage surrounded by some hungry-looking gremlins.

She almost screamed in fear for her sister.

But she had to think.

"What can I do?" She whispered to herself. She

didn't have a lot of time because she didn't know when the Gremlins planned to feast upon her sister. Lollipop saw a huge, round, boulder and pushed it to create a distraction. Once she did that all the Gremlins' focus went straight on that loud noise. They didn't know what it could've been so they ran to where they thought they heard the noise come from. Lollipop then sneakily ran to the Cage.

When she saw how scared Candypop looked she immediately tried to figure out the code but kept failing. Candypop had overheard the Gremlins saying the code. But her arms were tied and her mouth was taped up so Lollipop could barely understand, But Lollipop was running out of time. Lollipop used her senses and told Candypop to lick the tape. Candypop thought the idea was stupid but the denser the tape the less sticky it was. Eventually, Candypop got the tape off her lips and was able to say the code. Lollipop got CandyPop out of the cage and they had to run. They overheard the Gremlins coming back and had to move fast.

Candypop then signaled that the Gremlins were ahead. So they slowed down and tried to sneak but they had to catch Grimland gate before it closed. Candypop and Lollipop ran and got through the gate right before it closed. They saw the Gremlin Guss look at them and he and the other gremlins started dashing towards the two. The gate was already closed. Guss and the other gremlins were so close that they almost snatched both of them. Luckily Lollipop and Candypop were too fast. When Lollipop and Candypop got away they ran back to the Kingdom.

Guss and the Gremlins screamed in anger as they were in front of Grimland gate. They were devastated that they didn't catch them. The Gremlins went into the homes and had to eat their usual trashy food. They hoped that they would be able to have another opportunity to catch any candy people. Lollipop and Candypop finally got back into the Kingdom. Lollipop apologized to Candypop for pressuring her even when she knew Candypop didn't want to go.

"I am so sorry!" Lollipop said.

She promised that she would never disobey their parents again. Candypop accepted her apology and they finally got home. They got home super late and their parents were worried and wondering why they weren't home earlier. Lollipop looked at Candypop and was ready to take the blame for all of it, But Candypop came up with a fast lie so they didn't get in trouble.

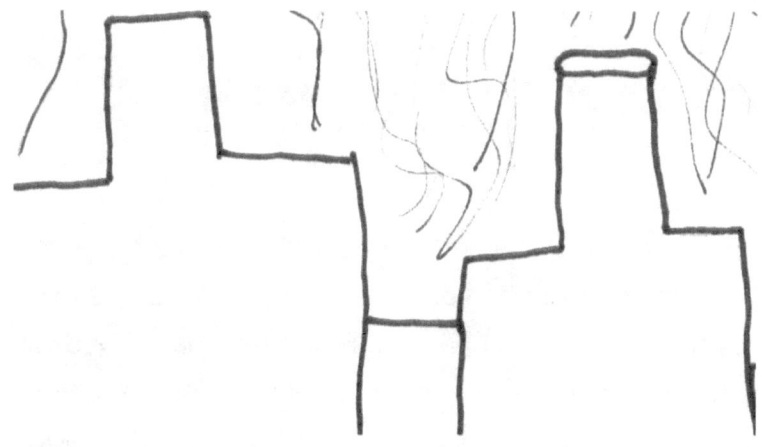

Cara Dawn

Olivia Summerlin

Rainbow On The Water

by Keira Collins

Once upon a time, it all started with a creek. A creek
that lacked man-made sounds and objects and was over-
flowing with nature. A beautiful clear creek that flowed with
a subtle yet ever-present sound of rocks being splashed
against. The moss on this creek's edges seemed to glow
with green, so vibrant it could have been from a mythical

forest. Birds chirped in the trees, making the creek feel happy yet calm. The air pushed through those trees as gracefully as a feather falling slowly down to land, without a single noise or sign of disturbance.

There was a lovely person that sat on the bank with their feet in the water looking at all the rocks, astounded by how smooth, perfect, and beautiful they are. Her jeans were rolled up as high as they'd go; slightly cutting off the circulation to her legs. Her shoes and socks were thrown to the side of the creek, most likely to be forgotten on the way back.

The lack of man-made sounds and objects, along with the smell of earth that floated through her nose made her happy and calm. Suddenly a deep voice rang through the air, it broke the tranquil and rural noises of the nature surrounding.

"Hey!"

The voice echoed through the creek, causing the fish to swim away and it made the rocks shake as it amplified because of the dips in the creek's edges. She fell back from surprise, splashing water all over her clothes that she had been desperately trying to keep dry.

"Ahh! What the heck do you want?" She yelled in response, slightly louder than she had meant to.

"Pfft, sorry to disturb you. My name is Anthony. But the water is black, behind you. Did you pour something in it or...?" He was a guy about her age and fit the description of tall, dark, and handsome, to a tee. He seemed like a nerdy guy but he was also super handsome and was probably hit on a lot because of it. He had gorgeous glowing green eyes that shone like emeralds as the light bounced off of them. His emerald eyes paired perfectly with his dark black hair that fluffed in all directions magnificently. He had a tired and blank expression on his face, much like the ones her friends held after all getting high together. Ash then responded bleakly,

"Oh uh, my name's Ash, and what in the world are you talking about; I have been sitting here for a minute just sitting here. I don't have anything to even pour in the water." Ash turned around to face the water only to see a deep, black, unnatural shadow flowing on top of the water. Though they seemed to be mixed she could still see the separation of the two substances. The dark liquid was also slightly tinted with a rainbow of colors.

"Oil?" She wondered out loud, though it was obvious what it was.

"Well, duh," Anthony remarked making Ash feel a bit dumb, "Want to come with me and we can see where it's coming from?"

Ash sat up eager but weary and followed Anthony. They walked alongside the clear creek and made sure not to trip over the roots that had gone haywire up and out of the dirt. The birds had flown away synchronized with each other, probably noticing the oil as well as Ash and Anthony had. Suddenly, they heard people talking; not just talking, talking as if they were being sneaky or not doing what they are supposed to.

"Hurry up and pour it before someone sees us!" a man said, rushed and worried sounding. Ash guessed that whoever he was talking to was doing all the work.

"Yeah, yeah I'm pouring it," another man said, sounding similar, but he had a strained tone to his voice as if he was doing a lot of physical labor. Ash and Anthony continued around the creek soon seeing two people pouring a huge container of oil into the creek rushing desperately to get it done.

Anthony ran up (almost tripping over an upturned root) and said, "Hey, you can't do that! This is a Wildlife sanctuary! I'm calling the police!"

His tone was weird, almost as if he was pushing fake emotions like an actor would in a play or movie. Ash pushed it out of her thoughts. He was just surprised about the people pouring the oil, right?

The men jumped in shock and threw the oil can to the side, which ended up rolling into the creek and causing the water to become more drenched in oil. The clear creek

Ka'Naisha Green

was no longer clear; it was murky black; though the water and oil hadn't mixed because, well they can't...you know... science. The men bolted quickly towards the parking lot close to the creek, which was nothing more than a dirt patch that someone decided to park in one day, and then was called a designated parking lot for the creek.

One of the men yelled, "Oh! Get to the car before they take a picture of us!"

Ash and Anthony then followed the men to the parking lot. Ash started to feel her feet being cut as she ran across the dirt and rocks and looked down, her feet were bare and rocks were cutting into the bottom of her feet. She had forgotten her shoes by the creek. The men got in their car and drove off. But before they got out of sight, Ash got a picture of their license plate, just in case. Anthony had called the local Busiek police station and a woman answered.

"Busiek County Police Department, what seems to be your problem?"

The woman's tone was already annoyed, and said,

Chloe Hwang

"Just get this over with." She had been bombarded by prank calls and old people asking where their underwear was all day.

"Two men were pouring a bunch of oil into the creek at Busiek park. We got a picture of the license plate if that helps." Anthony's eyes were big and his tone was shaky, probably from running. Ash herself was panting a bit herself though she wasn't using her air to talk like Anthony was.

"Oh um, the police department doesn't handle those kinds of things, you know we handle more important matters like robberies and violations of public property, et-cetera. Try the park rangers, maybe they can help out with that, you know because they are park rangers they deal with parks and stuff."

You know, for a police officer they're kind of rude, Ash thought to herself.

"What? Do you mean to tell me someone violating a wildlife sanctuary isn't a big deal? You would find their money if this was say, the Grand Canyon that's having oil poured into it. We have their license plate, isn't there a charge for illegally dumping oil?"

Ash heard his weird tone and thought, *There's that weird tone in Anthony's voice again, the one that sounds like an actor. Is it just how he talks or does he know some-thing he isn't saying? Maybe he just had seen the men before and didn't want to make himself sound guilty when he wasn't.*

"No, we can not. Try the park rangers or forget about the whole thing. Have a good day." *Beep.* She hung up on them.

Anthony and Ash stared at each other in awe and confusion, what were they supposed to do now? The park rangers wouldn't be able to do anything without any proof of them pouring it into the creek.

Ash jumped into her car and watched as Anthony circled through the woods and walked back towards the creek. She also had noticed there were no other cars in the parking lot other than hers and wondered how he got there. So many questions jumbled through her brain that she pushed them all aside and left to go home.

A month or two later, Ash thinks about going back to the creek but before she walks out the door, she slumps on the couch and she looks at the park's website. Mainly to see if there is anything she needs to look out for, such as bears, poisonous snakes, or loose cannibals, you know, the important things. She is scrolling through the page and her eye catches this heading, "Three Men Caught For Pouring Oil Into A Creek At A Park And Wildlife Sanctuary." There are three pictures underneath the heading...the two men from the creek weeks before, and that guy with gorgeous eyes, Anthony.

She skims through the article to see what all happened and why Anthony is involved in it. It reads, "Three men were recently caught illegally pouring oil in a creek. The two older men, Erik and Henry were pouring oil into the creek, and the minor, Anthony, had left to make sure no one was watching only to find a girl. In hopes to cover himself up, he ratted out his companions and almost got away with it. They, all three, were caught a week later at yet

Chloe Hwang

another creek and were arrested for illegally dumping oil at a wildlife sanctuary."

Ash thought to herself, *Wow, It all started with that creek. I thought he was on the opposite side. He is the one who pointed out the oil as if he was accusing me of pouring it into the creek. Clever...*

Ash went to the creek and walked barefoot along the creek which was still slightly tinted black with subtle shimmers of a rainbow, there were no fish in the creek, no animals at all, and the plants surrounding the creek had started to die. All the birds had all flown away, probably because of all the fish swimming away.

Ash began to think, *That needs to be cleaned up before all the animals around here die from water poisoning. Maybe if there were people involved in helping clean it, it would be fun.*

Ash thought for a while about this while picking wildflowers that she found near the woods and realized that there wasn't anyone she knew that would help clean it. No one was passionate about it like she was. Ash realized that she could clean it, she was passionate about it.

She rushed home and jumped on her computer to put together a volunteer group to help her clean up the local creeks and rivers. She threw together a website that said what she wanted to have done, how people could help her with it, along with her contact information of course. She then sat and waited for someone to contact her about cleaning the creeks.

Weeks passed and no one had contacted her about anything. No one even asked a question about what they would help out with or anything like that. She tried to make a TikTok page dedicated to funding and helping spread the idea of cleaning the creeks. She posted daily about cleaning up the creeks, rivers, and wildlife areas and also through random fun facts in there to make it more appealing to others. More weeks passed and no one had said anything, no questions, no comets, no nothing. Not even hate comments. She was losing hope in finding people to help her out with cleaning the creeks.
This is how it is, I guess.

Ash closed her computer solemnly to move on to working on her homework. She had to write an essay about the economy of the 1500s for History class and had math homework to do after.

Ash sighed to herself,

"Heh...and to think, it all started with a creek."

N'Dea Greenwood

The Wish of Mortality

Nicholas Fryer

Once upon a time, far within Acheron, the realm of war, atop a scorched hill, a tired elf sat alone. He was covered in soot and ash, yet the elf's white hair and pale skin were still visible. The elf had a godly glow as he sat watching the battle below him. Around his neck hung on a cord of golden thread an amulet with the three different colored jewels embedded in it shining in the afternoon light.

He was the mightiest warlock in all the realms, from honing his skills for eons against other gods. The elf became bored with being the god of destruction. Wars won, buildings destroyed, and people killed became tiring. The elf was known as Luran, he traveled across the abyss and the nine hells for entertainment. Acheron was entertaining once when people could challenge him. Within Acheron now, none had enough power or gall to oppose Luran. There was no challenge here for him, no force to stop him, and no drive for him to continue.

Luran had not left Acheron in centuries, it was isolated compared to the other realms. News from the other realms was hard to come by let alone confirm. After the day's battles were done he left for the pub, for he wished to learn news of the other realms.

The pub was an inactive lava tube in a small volcano that was hollowed out by dwarves decades ago. Inside it was intricately carved stone furniture lighted by magma flowing around it. Bickering, bosting, and songs of war were still everywhere around him as he ordered his drink.

"Barkeep," called Luran.

"Hello Luran, what would you like today?" asked the barkeep.

Conor Fryer

"A pint of mead," replied Luran.

As Luran drank his mead, two large orcs entered the bar still in uniform from the battle. The orcs' uniforms were torn, missing armor plates, showing their dark green skin beneath. The orcs ordered their drinks and while they waited on the barkeep, they began to speak.

"Ghag, have you heard there is a god that became mortal?" said the first orc.

"Are you sure there is Nuk?" asked Ghag.

"Asmodeus did it to the god," Nuk replied as they picked up their drinks and wandered to a table.

Luran contemplated what he heard for a few weeks. The thought of losing immortality was intriguing. It would allow me to have a challenge in battle. No longer would I be the victor of the encounters. I could be defeated, and have to come back again. He considered the source of his inspiration and decided to leave Acheron to confirm this rumor. He used The Amulet of the realms to open a gateway to the beast lands also known as the realm of idealized nature. In doing so The Amulet started to glow as a vortex surrounded by spiraling runes opened. There the gods had eyes and ears everywhere. No rumor would go unheard, where better to learn the truth.

Once Luran arrived he went to speak with his old friend who lived deep within the forests of the beast lands. She was the queen of the forests known as Mielikki. Luran walked along the gravel path to her house. At the end of the path sat a Rare and unusually large tree. She had chosen this as the place to make her home.

It was the tallest and only dragon tree in miles around,

towering over the rest. The tree smelled sweet and softly of amber. A small river of blood-red sap flowed down from the tree's bark. Far above Luran was a small house, among the branches and surrounded by clusters of fruit.

After hours of climbing, Luran reached the top of the trunk. The house was in the center of this being made of the branches interwoven together. It was surrounded by a lake of the blood-red sap dripping from other branches that grew even farther above.

Luran walked atop the sap, as only water walkers of his power could, to reach the porch of the house. After he pounded on the door an elven lady garbed in hunter green as if she had just come from a hunt exited the house. She was startled to see who had sought her out in her secluded home.

"Oh, hello Luran, what a pleasant surprise, I haven't seen you in centuries," said Mielikki.

"Mielikki, I need some information. You are the only one who would be able to tell me the truth of any rumors. From what I overheard In the bar, there are rumors that some- one became mortal, all their immortality lost, truly mortal. How did it happen?" asked Luran.

"It is true. The god made Asmodeus angry by killing some guards. So he turned him, mortal. Why do you want to know?" said Mielikki.

"I am tired of life as a god, for nothing challenges me anymore, I'm searching for an adventure that will give me a reason to live. Mortality might be such an adventure," said Luran.

After a few hours of catching up, Luran left for the nine hells once more. Luran using The Amulet of the Realms re-

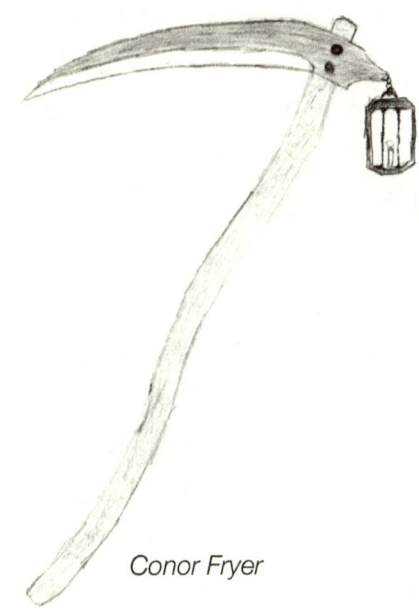

Conor Fryer

opened a vortex through space-time, though to Avernus the first layer of hell. A few hours after arriving Luran located the way to the second layer of hell Dis. Once Luran located Asmodeus's castle in Dis he entered. A guard Stopped Luran upon his entry.

"Halt! State your business, sir," said the guard.

"I am here to speak with Asmodeus about a deal," replied Luran.

"You can not enter, no weakling is allowed to see Asmodeus," said the guard.

"I am Luran, I defeated Tharizdun the chained god," boomed Luran.

As he quaked in fear the guard open the door, allowing Luran to pass into Asmodeus's chamber. The chamber was a red and gold-clad room covered from wall to wall in mounted skulls. In the center of the chamber sat Asmodeus upon a gold and ruby throne. Asmodeus was an extraordinarily tall being with red skin and glowing red eyes with two sets of horns. He held a ruby skull attached to a four-foot-tall claw-like rod.

"Who Dares enter my Chambers without my permission?" bellowed Asmodeus.

"My dear friend, you know it is I, Luran. I've been a God as long as you have you know who I am," responded Luran. "I have come to beg you for a favor. I have heard in the forest that you can remove immortality from even a god."

"Indeed I have but it always comes at a cost you should know this by now," responded Asmodeus.

Luran considered this for a moment before he replied, "So will you explain the cost or must I make an offer."

"Luran you must give me something of immense value, something I do not already possess."

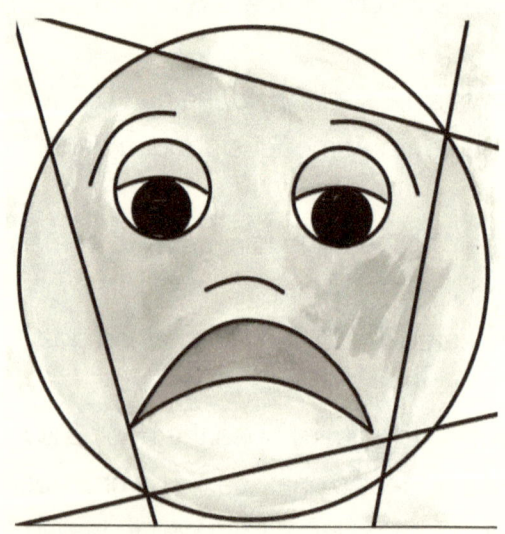

Iliana Domenech

"But we are both gods, so I, unlike you, do not keep things and possessions. I have traveled the realms and I seek knowledge and experience. That is why I have grown bored with my existence. You have collected many items of wealth that I see here in your chambers. So how could I have something to offer you?"

"You have gathered objects of immense power and value to increase your strength. One of those may suffice. What would you be willing to relinquish in exchange for mortality?" countered Asmodeus.

"I have traveled through many realms and I have collected a few such items. But who knows what you would deem worthy. So I will make a deal here as I stand before you, if you can see something that you desire, request it. I want to be able to walk out of here a mortal man," muttered Luran.

"I see, You have many objects of immense power and value. Though The Amulet you are wearing may suffice for the arrangement," retorted Asmodeus.

Luran bowed his head as he considered the request. This is The Amulet of the realms. One of my most valued and treasured possessions as it allows me to travel between the realms freely. If I gave this up not only would I lose immortality but my ability to travel. Would I find what I truly want? Luran pondered. He raised his head and looked Asmodeus in the eyes.

"Asmodeus I will accept your condition. I will trade The Amulet of the realms for my mortality. I will walk out of here as a mortal, ready to seek the next adventure," offered Luran.

"Hand me the amulet and you shall be given mortality and live as a mortal," said Asmodeus as he sealed the deal.

Luran handed over the Amulet of the realms to Asmodeus. Suddenly he felt weak as his power drained from him, and a red light flowed around him. When his transformation was completed, his existence as a god was erased from the memories of all mortals. No longer would he be remembered as a god, only a destructive warlock. Slowly he turned around and faced Asmodeus. As a mortal, he felt what it was like to be standing in the presence of a god.

"Thank you, Asmodeus. The deal is complete. I no longer am your equal as a god, and I can begin a new adventure, " said Luran.

"Though you may no longer be a god, we are still equal. I hope you will find your future adventures as a mortal fulfilling."

Asmodeus opened up a gateway using the amulet of the realms, to Averniuos, allowing Luran safe passage to the first layer of Hell. Luran stepped through the portal as simply an elf.

Luran wandered through Averniuos searching for the exit to the mortal realm. Without his godly power, the path was no longer visible. He could hear fighting in the distance as he traveled. He decided to follow the sounds in hopes it would lead to the exit. It was the logical way to travel.

Once he reached the battle, he did his best to avoid the combatants. They were numerous and covered the hillside. He strode along the edge, trying to continue his progress, but there were so many. The way ahead was blocked. Without the Amulet, he was reduced to mere walking, no more portals.

He stopped to rest, at the bottom of a hill. Loran watched the battle in front of him. They fought with clanging swords, whistling arrows, and fireballs lit the sky. There was no-where to escape the thunderous sounds. Now was the time to start his mortal life and join the battle.

Luran ran into the battlefield striking down foes as he went. He elegantly sliced through many foes before they could even realize what was going on around them. After killing more than thirty foes Luran got stabbed in the leg by a spear.

After the day's battles were done he attempted to mend his wounds in a small tent set up at the base of the mountain. They were proving difficult to mend, some soldiers he was fighting with helped him mend them. He enjoyed the thrill of the battle even through the pain.

Though he was still injured he fended off some of the foes. He was no match for their large numbers, he was over-whelmed in minutes. An arrow ripped through the sky, striking Loran in the head. The mortal elf fell, killed instantly. No longer the god of destruction, the warlock elf died alone.

Descendants of Aqüeybaná

Damien Marrero

Once upon a time, I woke up at my old apartment in Orlando, Florida. I did my routine to get ready for the school day and then headed out the door with my taller twin brother Enrique. He was about 5' 10" with dark brown hair and even darker eyes. I was shorter, around 5 feet tall, and had darker brown hair, so dark it looked black with hazel eyes. We walked in complete silence to the bus stop, because we were still tired.

We come from a magic-born family, and it was our first ancestor Aqüeybaná who discovered magic in another dimension.

We kept our distance from the other kids at the bus stop for a while until the earthquake came. Luckily for us, it lasted for a few seconds. I already heard the other kids blaming us for it and Enrique got furious.

An aftershock came and lasted two times longer than the first earthquake, and a blue portal emerged above us.

"What is happening!? Juan, you have the magic totem on; suppress it with your magic!"

I froze. "I-I do not know how." That was all I managed to say. Everyone started standing up and screaming. The only thing I remember before we got sucked in was my dog running to us talking even though he is a dog, incapable of speaking.

I woke up in a barren desert. I stood up to look around, but I found nothing except for my dog Steel. I ran to my dog and went on my knees and started shaking him up and yelled, "Steel, wake up! Steel, you have to wake up! We need to find Enrique!"

"Master, he is fine. He is probably buried under the dunes. Now please let me sleep." He dozed back to sleep. Except he spoke. I fell backward and started stuttering.

"Y-You s-speak!?" I was so startled I forgot all about Enrique. While my tiny freakout was happening, I looked up and realized the clouds, sky, and sun were off. The atmosphere was blue, green, red, and purple jumbled together. The clouds looked like giant spirals that were oddly very black. The sun was the oddest because there were two gigantic blue suns.

"I wonder why you are surprised? Anyway, the only way to find him is with a magic spell. I do sense a lot of mana in you." My dog stood up. "All you have to do is first release a bit of your mana and then repeat after me, magic art: article one, gust storm."

Nathen Jones

I first let a bit of my mana out, which released a lot of wind to course around my body along with sand, then repeated, "Magic art: article one, gust storm!" The extensive system of wind took all the sand, and the sand just floated up above me. I waved my hand up, and it looked like the sand had just got flown away to space. Then, there was a yell above, and I looked up. It was Enrique falling!

"Hey, Lil brother, can I have a little help, please!?" My brother cried out, and then I used the same spell to carry him up the air and slowly planted him below me on the barren rock surface.

I ran down to him and helped him up. "You ok? Also, where are we?" I asked. I did not find a town or village nearby. I just saw barren rock instead of sand.

"I do not even know. Wait." Enrique noticed Steel and patted his head. "What are you doing here? Wait! Are you not sick!? Why did you follow us here!?" My brother asked so many questions I even got dizzy.

"Look, we do not have time for this, Enrique. We need to find everyone. If only we knew where we were. I wish we had a map!"

My dog somehow grinned. "Well, there is a magic spell. All you have to say i-" My dog stopped mid-sentence and ran.

I heard noises myself. It sounded like people but they were speaking a language I didn't even know. It did not sound like a human. I tried to hide but there was nowhere to go. And so Enrique and I got captured and knocked out.

We woke up in a palace of what looked like obsidian. The question was, how would anyone obtain this much obsidian? I looked around once more and saw Enrique, Wally, Kj, and Chloe. The kids at the bus stop were there! Then there was Steel on a royal throne without a crown, acting as the king. I tried to speak, but I could not for some reason. I tried to move my body but could not. I was the only one awake, but immediately after I struggled, I could move and speak again.

"Steel, what is going on! Tell me now!" I shouted at the top of my lungs.

"One, I am not Steal. I am king Arberius the fifth. I just happened to be in the human world as a cub and found you the real rulers of this dimension. I would not have it, though. Although I do appreciate you as my servants, not masters, I will let you live but not your friends." *Oh no, he was the king!* "I will let your friends live if you do a little quest for me. Here is the one rule: You must not quarrel with your friends, and you must work together. I hear from my spies that you have fought. You are stripped from your magic and banished. Also, you must make sure everyone stays alive. That is all."

Those were oddly strange rules. Why would the king want us to work together?

"I will train you and Enrique for two weeks. May the games, I mean quest, begin now!" We teleported to some coliseum and, for two weeks, we trained as hard as we could.

Enrique had the magic of Terra, and I had the magic of Reality. Kj became a swordsman, Chloe had archery, and Wally was the healer. The canyons were where we had to go. After many fights with goblins and orcs, we made it to the crimson dragon.

"Now is our time. To our return!" I yelled to wake the dragon. We all screamed in agreement, and I put the dragon in a trance to think we were not here, and Chloe climbed to a ledge of rock and aimed at the horn of the dragon, for it was its weakness.

Enrique raised the earth the dragon was standing on. Then down so it could fall but it let its wings out and stayed in the air. My spell went away after that and then it started breathing fire to everyone.

"Chloe, Kj, Wally, watch out!" I warned and dodged the flames. Chloe released the arrow in midair and used her explosive quiver, and one of the horns broke off. "Just one more!"

"Juan, use that spell now!" Enrique ordered.

"Alright! Magic type: Reality! Article: 789, Reality shift!" I transformed into a silver dragon bigger than the

Barbara Walters

crimson dragon. Everyone ran to safety. I hit the dragon with my claws and then grabbed it and threw it to one of the walls. I pinned it to the wall and opened my dragon mouth. A plasma beam as powerful as a solar flare started to warm up, then in point-blank range hit the dragon, obliterating it.

I shifted back to human form and fell to the ground. There was a hole in the canyon full of heat. "We won!" Enrique laughed.

We all laughed but the ground shook. The battle was not over. "Look, the canyon is collapsing," Chloe warned.

I saw a crimson eye then the canyon was ripped open by the crimson dragon. It was as big as Mount Everest! It had tons of armor around its horn and its body. Suddenly, like a phantom, some random person with a hood appeared. The person fought the dragon so hard, sometimes taking a few punches and fire. Then, reality distorted, and it disappeared.

"I knew this would happen, Juan. And yes, it is me, Kind Arberius the Fifth. Well, I see you are in your primitive human forms. I will return you to your dimension now."

The blue portal, the same one from the bus stop, appeared above us. "Thank you for saving this dimension and, if you come back, I will consider bringing your family back to the throne. Arberius bid us farewell.

I said my farewells too, and our regular lives came back. It was happily ever after, more or less.

Janell Thomas

6 All Mixed Up

Cheetos, The Skinny Kid

Ryan Chaplin

Cheetos, the skinny kind.
Guess how many calories they're combined.
Cheetos, the skinny kind.
Yes, they are quite divine.
Cheetos, the skinny kind.

Call the hotline.
Where's his hairline?
Cause these Cheetos,
Yeah the skinny kind,
Will have me gone in no time.
Tell me the calories combined.

Chee TOU! Chee TOU! Like a mosquito.
This is how my heart responds to Cheetos.

Sound

Desyiah Simmons

Boom Boom! Clap! My favorite music is rap.
Because the beat is like my heart,
And the words are a map,
To the rhythm in my lap.

There is no reason for a nap when
You are your own favorite song.
And there's no way I'm wrong
because it didn't take me long to

Notice that I'm strong I feel like I always belong.
That is how cool you become when,
You are your own favorite song.

Vicky Flores

The Broken Board

Jeffrey Mueller

We broke a board on our balcony
It just kind of snapped.
Me and my brother can't go out there anymore
So we decided to call the office to fix the problem

And this is where it gets dumb.
Nobody picked up so my mom went there herself
And this is what they said it is our problem to fix it
Even though they own the building

So we did nothing about it and just left it there to rot
It was a couple of weeks ago when this story took its
course.
We called some more just the same response
So we decided to just leave and do nothing about it.

That hole is still here to this day and that's the dumbest
thing about it.

Ka'Naisha Green

How The Car Crashed

Jeremiah Chisolm

VROOM as the black BMW going 50,
And 35 miles per hour,
As the police chasing the black BMW,
HONK as the police tell the person.

Pullover and then… BAM the person,
Driving the BMW had crashed the car
Into a tree. As the police got out of the car,
And saw 3 people that passed away.

In a blink of an eye, The police call paramedics,
And… two people were killed and the driver,
Was alive looking devastated.
Then WEE WOO paramedics came,

To get the dead bodies. The driver got,
Arrested then at the court the driver had
Been sentenced to life in prison for no parole.
Then BAM the judge said the court dismissed.

Sounds

Khordae Parker

Paper crinkles,
Popcorn that pops,
Plane crash,
People tinkle,

Bombs go bang boom.

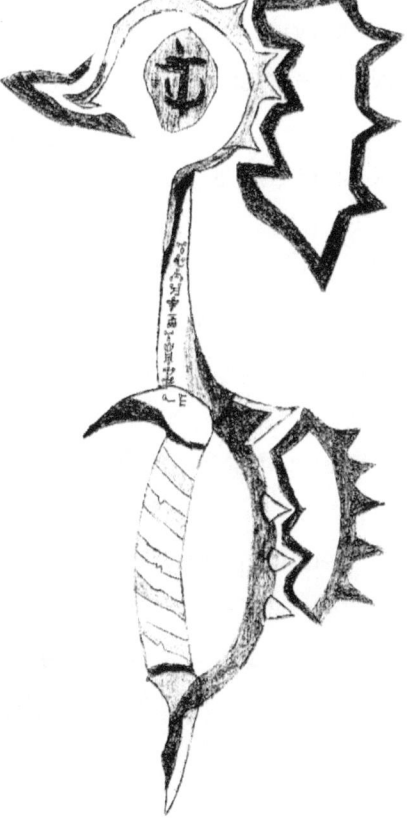

BOOM!

Jordan Easley

BOOM! Goes the fireworks,
Up into the air, it goes,
You hear it and feel it go…
BOOM! Can't you see it?
BOOM! Goes the dynamite,
With all of its might
It goes and explodes,
You're far away yet you still hear…
BOOM! Can't you see it?

Cash

Brooke Cumbee

It is 2021.
That means we have phones that do everything.
Most people now-a-day only carry their phones.
No one even carries cash anymore.

"Can I have $10 bucks?"
"Sure," then proceeds to Cashapp her $10 dollars.
The need for cash is not there anymore
Unless you're weird or old,
Then you might carry cash.

The satisfaction of getting handed a crisp new bill
Has now changed to the satisfaction
Of getting the notification:
Notification - mom venmoed you
$50 dollars "for your chore money."
Cash has moved to the hall of fame.

Brooke Cumbee

The Nurse

Mely Flores

I'm in the white room,
White sheets,
Rusty pillows.
The door opened as the nurse came in.

Saying my greetings to her while she takes care of me,
But giving me a gift.
I told her to thank you and she told me she loves me,
I didn't say I love you back though.

The gift stayed on my lap, I looked at it
Like it was something normal.
I heard a shot,
Screaming,
And the pain in people's voices.

"What happened?" I asked but nobody that was there.
The door opened hoping that it was the nurse
It was but turns out she was bad,
Physically and mentally.

Ka'Naisha Green

Thing's to Hear about Me

Omari Jenkins

Things that y'all are ready to hear about me.
This is poetry about me and the things that
Y'all are ready to hear about me.
The thing I like to do most is play the game.

And that always feels the same.
I also like to play sports,
And I also use to build forts.

And I got a lot of skins on Fortnite,
And I like to ride dirt bikes.
I bought some shoes last week,
And they coming on Sunday
And I got the red jordans 5s,

So I can wear them and look fly.
I like to play 2k sometimes,
One of my favorite songs is drumline.
And the artist that made it is Glock nine.

And he's about to get out of jail sometime.
He was a good artist,
But he did some bad things.
This is the end of the poem, so
Have a nice day.

Coffee

Nicholas Fryer

Coffee!
Coffee!
I would kill for coffee.
Give me coffee now.

No, not Starbucks,
Their coffee is bad.
And if you like it you're bad with legs,
The only way to go is a breath wish.

I want some breath wish.

Vicky Flores

Oh, Sam

Miguel Ferguson

As agile as a Monkey
Sam climbed the tree.
Fell on his back,
His mom thought that his
Bones cracked.

Sam laughed it off and said,
The sound was a branch.
His mom told him to not
To climb that tree again.
But Sam did not hesitate.

He climbed the tree again.
And again.
And again.

Sam was bad.

Christopher Lopez

Love be Danged

Micayah Seabrook

On the bathroom floor, she sat,
Gazing at that which was black.
She brushed her fingers over the flat.
When she touched it she stepped back,
Then emerged a wolf pack.
She screamed and screamed trying to run away.
But all that screaming couldn't save her anyway.

From far away
"Grrrrr" growled a stray
That watched his love get taken away.
Leaving his home as the wolves who
Killed his love strutted away.
He vowed to take revenge one day.
He came back down the mountain
that he passed on his way,
And went to the house where
The body of his love lies.
He cried and cried all day.

Ulises Oliva

But it didn't seem to soothe the pain.
Once he got himself together and
Buried her where they stayed.
He then put himself to sleep with his love
In hopes of someone finding him one day.

Oh, Where the Flower Grows

Micayah Seabrook

Oh, where the flower grows.
Where does the flower grow?
East, West, North, South.
It might be from the South
There is nothing but trash and debris there.

It might be from the East where
There are shootings and gang rivalries.
It might be from the North where
There are rich snobby kids.

It might be from the south where it is
Hard to find your next meal.
We might never know where the flower grew.
Where is the flower now?

Ka'Naisha Green

Where the flower grew doesn't matter
What matters is where the flower is now.
The flower is no longer a flower
From the East, West, North, Or South.

What matters now is if it
Grew to blossom or to stay
In the slums of where it grew from.

We will never truly know if the
Flower bloomed or not.
There are thousands of f
Fowers but only a few
Get to bloom to their fullest potential.
Be the few who bloom.
Oh, where the flowers bloom.

Vicky Flores

I Want To Play Football

Malachi Johnson

I like football and I like basketball
And everything that makes them so great
Is the team,

Being a football player
One day is my dream.
I know being a football player
Will make me strong,
And I know I will have to
Play hard and long.

And playing hard and long
Will make me smarter at the game.
And being smarter at the game
Will keep me on the team.

And that's all I really want.

Cara Dawn

Leaves

Logan Bonilla

Leaves are as light as a feather,
They blow upon the wind catching
A ride into the unknown,
They fall off trees in fall like hair.

Falling from a person's head,
And when it's springtime they grow back
Like flowers, blooming on trees,
They are a creative yet simple thing,

Leaves are like when we lose our first tooth.
It's gone for a while but
Before you know it, its back.

They're vital to trees like
How food is to us.

Kiera Collins

On a Stormy Hight

Leah Reconco

On a stormy night, I often wonder,
Why am I blessed to be alive?
I have done so many bad things,
I shouldn't have lied.

On a stormy night, I realized,
I shouldn't have to cry; judge myself,
Instead of crying every night,
I should be thanking you every time.

On a stormy night, I thank God for all,
The people of my time, the people of my time,
Should be thanking the one almighty instead,
Of wasting their limited time.

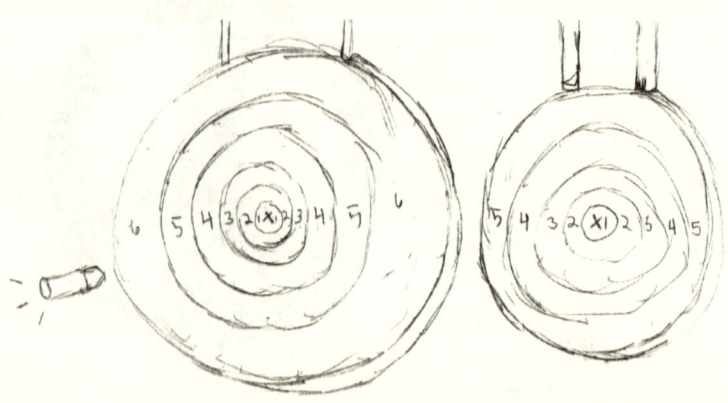

Christopher Lopez

On a Sunny Morning

Leah Reconco

On a sunny morning, I wonder,
Why you chose us; why you loved us,
You were perfect but you paid the price.
On a sunny morning, I cry out your name

And "say speak to me please",
But how are you going to speak to me
If I don't speak to you?
We, humans, ask why there are sick people,
But that is a cry for you to seek more for him.

On a sunny morning, I ask for understanding.
And when he gives me something,
That needs me to be understanding.
I ask "why did you do that"?
If I asked for understanding, not a situation
Where I need understanding.

Then he feels sad and alone
And then we wonder
Where did his presence go?

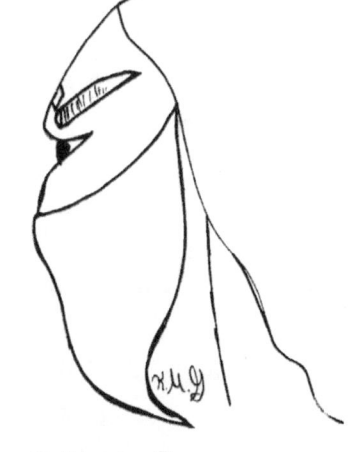

Ka'Naisha Green

Food

Keira Collins

I was hungry today.
So I went to the store.
I looked and I got what
I needed, nothing more.
Before I tell you,

I must include
Something important,
I am vegan.
But when I got home,
I had bacon on the stove.

Jayda Brown

I Am So Bored

Kamari Johnson

I am so bored.
The class I'm in is as dry as the desert.
This classroom is so big
A hippo could fit in it.

The binder made a big "boom" sound,
When it dropped on the ground.
The trees are dancing as
The wind is blowing them outside.

Golf

Jose Aguilar Avila

Oh, so boring.
Don't know why people play it.
There are other sports in the world.
Why play the most boring one?

I get it, it might be relaxing.
But really?
Out of all the sports,
The most talentless one.

It's an old person game.
I bet a turtle could
Get a
Hole in one.

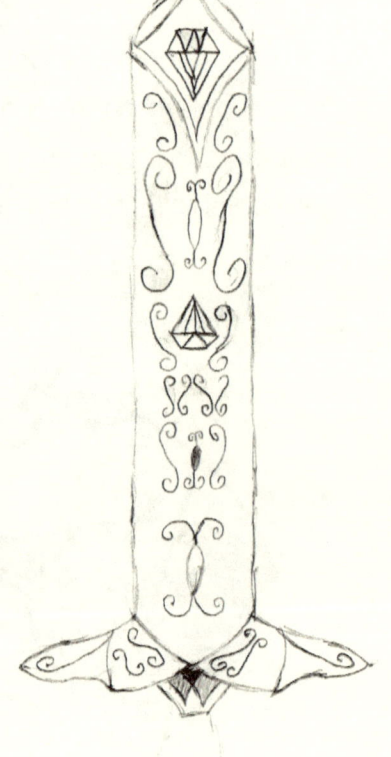

Conor Fryer

Snow

Jose Aguilar Avila

Oh I wish it would snow,
But it's the middle of summer.
Plus it wouldn't snow at all,
Cause here in the south,
It's like it's banned.

The one time it happened,
I couldn't go outside.
My parents got mad.
And I got
Snow in my butt.

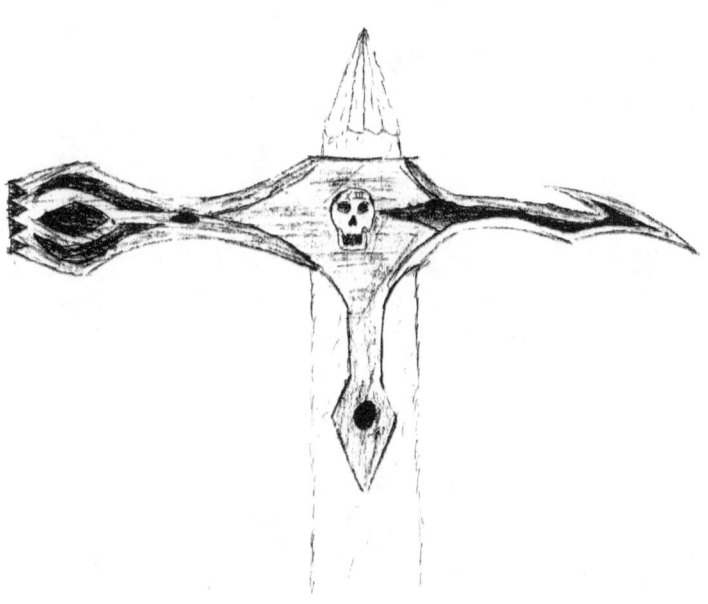

Conor Fryer

The Man From Peru Who Lost His Shoe

Jayda Brown

Once there was a man from Peru who lost his shoe.
Without a clue, he didn't know what to do,
So he cried all night long like a fool.
Then he stood on a stool and saw the color blue.

Then he was no longer a fool who lost his cool.
And while he sat on the stool he admired the shoe,
Blue was the one thing he knew that kept him cool.
The next day he remembered the shoe turned blue.

Blue, he knew, was the color of his shoe.
So he looked for his shoe sure to find a clue,
On how he knew that it was a blue shoe.
Then he remembered the day he had the shoe

That he had a blue toe from blue glue that he saw
And was tempted in aww that he saw glue that was
Blue, so he took off his shoe in order to put the blue
Glue on his toe and the left the shoe
Because the blue toe was new.

Spaceship I Was On:

Jameson O. Perkins

Siting I was,
My new spaceship I was given,
Walking around I was,
Think nothing bad I was,
Then rock hit our ship,

Ka'Naisha Green

Big the rock was,
The janitor and I ran to the life pods,
A bucket full of bubbly water he had,
Shot out of the ship and onto a deserted planet.

Once landed we walked for days,
Thirsty I was so I asked for some water,
Confused he lookod, "Yes," he said,
The bucket was empty when I finished,
We Found a town.
Needed to go to the bathroom I must,
I told the janitor, puke water I did,
Came out of the bathroom with water on face,
Janitor and I found a new ship, walked onto it

I did, and down I fell, and hit the ground
And that was it.

Bright As A Flower

Deviasia Jackson

I am as bright as a flower.
I am as bored as coming to school.
I am as tired as a sloth.
I am as cute as a panda.

Deviasia is kind and beautiful.
She is smart, she is smart.
She is bright, she is a cutie.
She is always tired, Deviasia.

Chloe Hwang

Glow Stick

Darilynn Caballero Garcia

When you snap a glow stick
And it starts to glow,
Do you ever wonder
How long it takes to stop?

If you refill the glow stick
Will it work again?
If you paint a canvas with a
Glow stick, will it glow?

Wandering in an art museum
Seeing well-painted artworks,
A canvas that was painted
With a glow stick is there.

You start to wonder;
How'd that get there?

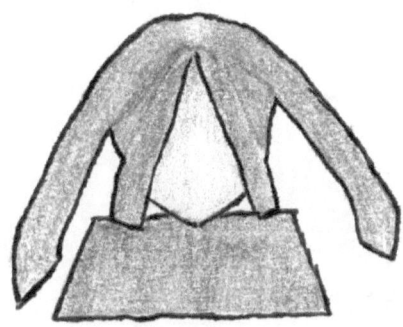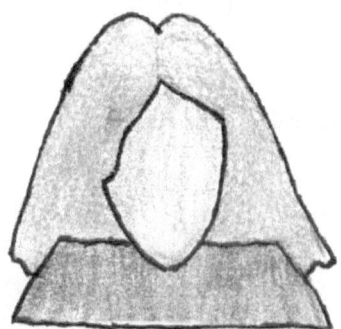

Vicky Flores

Bullied

Denise Morales Martinez

His name was Jeffrey,
Ran into the woods one night,
Afraid and alone.
Surrounded by darkness.

The voices comforted him,
They offered him a deal he couldn't refuse...
Had now been missing for years,
Was later found by a tree.

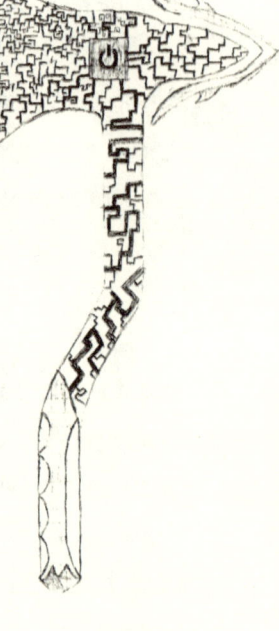

Bloody clothes face filled with terror,
Had been miss treated for so long.
Been punched and kicked,
Who would have thought they'd find him here.

Ka'Naisha Green

Oh poor little boy, hanging.
Jeffrey had completed his part of the deal,
For the body hanging wasn't him but was his old bully.
What an ugly fate.

He was only 12.

A Cloudy Chill Day

Imani Wolfe-Macanic

Old cloudy days chilly as ice,
May you please be bright as light
And let it be as hot as the sunny
Summer day?

Old cloudy days as chilly as ice,
I know you hear me calling you out.
Please hear what I have to say.

Oh cloudy chilly day, you need a break
From all that icy feeling, and let it be as
Sunny as the beach during the summer.
Be happy, don't be sad like the grinch!

Oh understand that there's plenty more
Than to be sad and bitter on a
Cloudy, chilly day
As ice their things you can do just
Get up your feet and be happy love.

I thought would love a lovely break.
Just take one and you will be happy as
People having fun at the beach.
Just hear me out, it's a good thing to do.

Cara Dawn

Hard Choices

Dante Cota

If you were to choose between
Vanilla or chocolate
Which will you choose?
You love vanilla but
Chocolate sounds good to you,
And you also might want strawberries too.
Why does it have to be so hard to choose?

Would you rather have
Fun now and be busy later
Or be busy and have fun with layers.
In some situations,
It might be hard to lose
But why does it have to be
So hard to choose?

When you choose one over the other
Do you ever wonder
What would happen if
You choose the other?

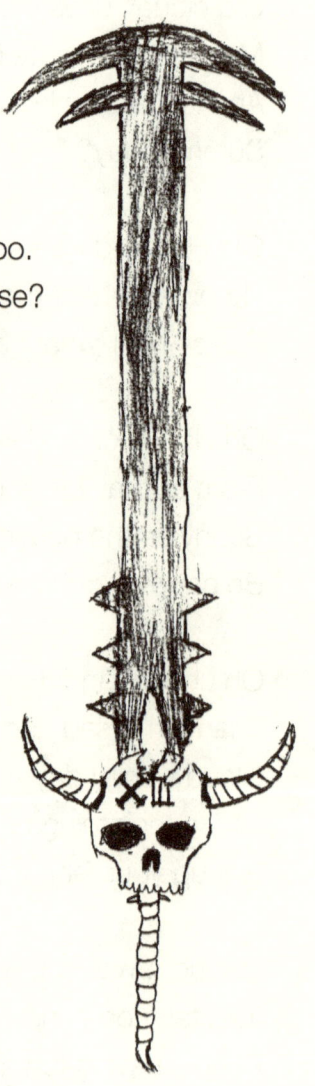

Conor Fryer

What if you had a nice warm shower,
Or what if you had gotten
Struck by thunder.
Why does it have to be so hard to choose?

Why is it hard for me to choose
When I could be buying a pair of shoes.
With the shoes, I can walk moonwalk
But what if I fall on the sidewalk?
Why does it have to be
So hard to choose?

Is this normal for you and me?
Is it to be or is it just me?
Why am I not certain?
Why am I not divisive?
Can someone please tell me
Why does it have to be
So hard to choose?

Conor Fryer

Do You Think?

Shyann Owens

Do you think school is just somewhere to go
Between the afternoon and evening?
Do you think home is just somewhere to go
After coming from school?

Do you think School is like broccoli?
Do you think you're like a fish in a tank
Swarming around when you're in school?

Have you ever wanted to do
Nothing more than lay down?
Have you ever wanted to do
Nothing more but just to take
Over the world sometimes?

Have you ever thought about
How hard it would be to become president?
Have you ever thought about
Whether presidents eat McDonalds or not?

Did you ever get mad at someone
For doing the bare minimum?
Did you ever text the wrong person on accident?
Did you ever get called someone else's name?

Did you ever space out and
Start thinking about food?

When you look at stars do you I
Look for the big dipper?
When you're eating do you always
Need something to drink?

When you lose in a game,
Do you feel sadness and maybe
More anger, too?
When you think about the sky,
Do you ever wonder why it's blue?

Conor Fryer

When Things Were Not As Hard

Oliva Reyes

When you were little, you did not get
Judged for what you did.
At an age so young, your head could
Never have thought what life would be like.

But now it all makes sense.
Why they always warned you about
Why you should enjoy your childhood.
Because in the future you would want to go back.

Life was easier because you didn't have to
Worry about school or over-stressing.
You did not have to worry whether your outfit was
On-trend or if you would get made fun of.

Life back then was full of love and care now
No matter what you do you will always be a
Failure in their eyes. If you answer them in their words.
The world is talking back, if you tell them the truth
Is also talking back. You can never be enough.

The World

Oliva Reyes

The world might look fine, but that
Is not true the world is dying
Gas is running out, natural fires are
Burning down the forests where many

Animals live. A lot of people in Cuba
Are being thrown out of their houses,
And being killed if they refused to leave.
In Afghanistan, girls are being kidnapped,

And used as sexual slaves to the leaders
That's wrong and not okay yes the world
Might be cruel but so are people,
The world Is dying as it goes and every day it
Gets worse when will it end and just be peaceful?

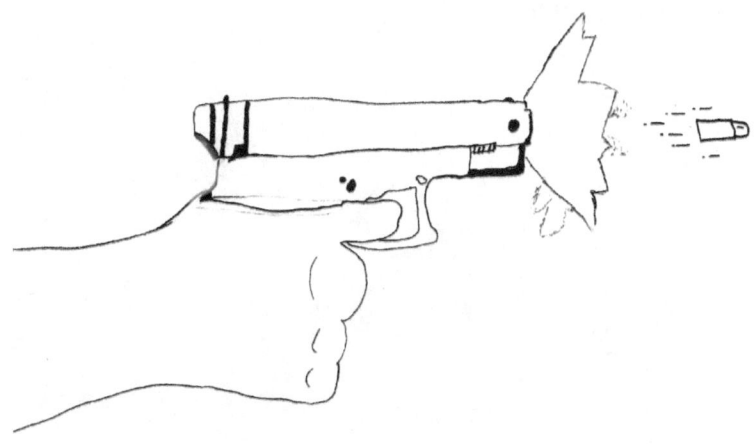

Brooke Cumbee

Candy

Denise Morales Martinez

Being surrounded by complete nothingness,
Watching as the light goes further and further away.
Desperately trying to hold on,
Yet something grabs you and
Pulls you down into the abyss.

Losing all your hopes and dreams,
All your pleasures and thoughts, lost.
Ever see a candy fall out of a kids hands,
So carelessly like they could just get another one.

Watching it fall and sink into
The bottom of the puddle,
Candy was a good friend.
That kid was a decent father.
That puddle, the ocean choked her out
Like she was nothing.

Vicky Flores

There's this little 8-year-old girl
Wondering where her best friend is.
At the bottom of the ocean,
But they don't know that.
Wondering why they haven't had a
Playdate in a while.

Why they haven't seen each other in a year.
And then be fed a lie.
A lie that stuck with that 8-year-old her whole life.
Until the day her mother said, "remember candy?"

No. no she doesn't because that
8-year-old girl blocked
"Candy," that name, from her mind.
She didn't want to remember
The friend that left her.

"She drowned."

Jameson Perkins

Invisible To The Eye

Gabrielle Myers

I am faceless.
I am invisible to the eye.
When I walk people do not hear
The clacking of my steps.
When I talk people can't hear
My endless stories.
I sit there, wondering if people will notice me.
If people can hear my cries for help.
I wonder, do they even know who I am?
Do they know the real me?

I just sit there. Alone. I have no friends.
No family. No one.
I just sit there alone.
Waiting for someone
to notice my sighs.
I am invisible to the eye.

Christopher Lopez

I am faceless.
When we are busy,
Everything entertains us,
But when we are bored,
The boredom is rigorous.
I can't focus for a long time,

But I know that when I am a grown-up,
I will do what I love.
And always grabbing the bull by the horns,
I'll never get bored and be always in comfort.
Even though adulthood might be stressful,
I will solve everything and live in plenty.

Brooke Cumbee

Olivia Sumerlin

7 Bending Minds

Soldiers

Trawley Harper

Transfer.
Join the army.
Do it if you Transfer
Join the army
Do it if you insist
But over here we drink Bud light's cold beer
You will feel like you are in the army if you aren't a recruit
For the sargents
The Soldiers
The Doctors too
Drink Bud Light beer it is the best thing you can do
Bud Light's beer is the best
After a day at war we crack open a can for a celebration
Drinking it you feel like you are a soldier at heart
Get you a beer and make you country proud

Give Up the Stamp of Approval

Ulises Oliva

Give people the stamp of approval
By using someone famous
Or well known
With the experience of course

"OMG MOMMY LOOK"
"IT'S SPIDERMAN IN A CHIPS COMMERCIAL"
"Can I get it pleaseee?"
"It's my favorite superhero"

Win someone over
By using someone famous
It Will make your case better
People would love it

Cara Dawn

Buy the Pink Car

Arson Clayton

This pink car is the new hot thing!

Even the very famous influential person says so.

This person is very trustful

That's why you should buy the pink car

The nice and not overrated pink car!

I would recommend this pink car

Because I'm THE very famous person!

I'm so cool and everyone loves me

So you should too.

And if you love me,

You should buy this great pink car

You could be cool like me

And I'm very trustworthy

So listen to me!

And buy the pink car

Mely Flores

Not a Good Fit

Ryan Chaplin

Catchy and humorous.
Short and memorable.
Not a good fit,
But a good eye-catcher.

The more catchy,
The more sales.
The cover of a book.
An eye-catcher.

A persona of humor
Persuades with a short message.
Memorized by a phrase,
Remarkable when catchy.

Get ring
before this happens to
You.

Chloe Hwang

Another Saying

Nicholas Fryer

Toyota says we're going places,
KFC has finger-licking good,
McDonalds has I'm loving it.

They all are awful,
None have class,
None have pazazz.

Disney has happiest place on earth,
Nike has just do it,
Pizza has no one can out pizzas the hut.

It all is boring,
People may like it,
Though it's all disgusting.

Best
Drink
Ever!!!!

Drink
Coke

Drink The Best Drink For The
Best You!!

Brooke Cumbee

Just Do It

Ulises Oliva

Just do it.
Everyone knows where it's from.
You say it,
You get called out.

"Was that the Nike catchphrase?"
Yes indeed it was.
Famously known,
Where ever you go.

It's just so catchy.
It's easily remembered.
It will get stuck in your head.
I'm lovin' it.

Denisev Martinez

There Were Protests

Brooke Cumbee

There were protests.
They were promoting the BLM.
Black Lives Matter…. The form of the black fist,
Promoted all over the country.

Flags flown with the fist
Flags flown to bring awareness
People of color are brought a
Feeling of comfort from the flag.
Seven minutes that brought new revolution.

Something that has meaning.
Something that is not known for violence.
Something that is about bringing justice.
Something that has brought justice.

Have you ever heard
Don't judge a book
By it's cover?
Well if you did, then
Don't make that mistake.

Denisev Martinez

Make it Easy

Brooke Cumbee

You want to stop using plastic.
"Just use metal."
But shouldn't we do more?
Shouldn't we try to actually try and do more than that?

We should not just do what is easiest,
We should try more.
Whatever is easiest is not the best.
Why not try starting petition for plastic outlaws?

It is not always best for simple solution.
Sometimes, it is best for the easiest.
But sometimes you should,
It all matters on the time

Chloe Hwang

Simple Solution

Jayda Brown

One day while walking on a road I spotted a frog.
This frog was holed in the road,
With no control over such an unfortunate occasion.
Lisa was in such a solemn mood before she
Saw this frog who had no choice but to stay holed up.

Lisa picked up the frog thinking that It would
Take her somewhere if she just followed.
The frog hopped happily without a thought but
Without this thought, he just hopped.

Lisa followed this mysterious frog inside
The fog that got deeper than a deep conversation.
Without a doubt It was an hour when
Lisa started getting sour, so she looked around.
There was a town. A town with a mysterious
Clown. This was no ordinary clown, indeed.

This clown had a frown because
No one came to his show.
Lisa saw the sign and thought,
"Oh No, I have to go to his show."
Lisa went inside and indeed had a night
With such an exciting life.

On Repeat

Victoria Flores

I like food and how tasty it is.
I like eating sweets throughout my childhood.
I like taking care of children even babies.
I like drawing pieces of little things.
I like the season spring.
I like hearing my cousin when she sings.
I like hanging out with friends of mine.

I like listening to a lot of the different types of music.
I like to listen to K-pop.
I like to listen to pop.
I like hearing a bit of musical theatre.
But what I love the most is them.

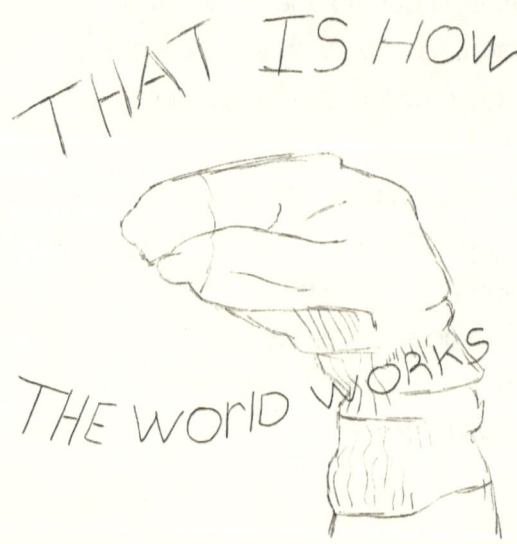

Denisev Martinez

Echoing In My Head

Arson Clayton

Buy this.
Buy that.
Buy buy buy!

Buy this amazing new car.
It's pink!
Pink car!
Pink Pink PINK!

This car is amazing.
An amazing car!
Omg, an amazing CAR?
Wow, an amazing carrrr!

You should buy this car.
Buy this car.
Buy buy buy!

Brooke Cumbee

Over and Over Again

Ryan Chaplin

Great sales.
Great deals.
Great products.
Great, Great, Great!

Helpful brand,
Helpful people.
Helpful, Helpful, Helpful!

Dangerous people,
Dangerous country.
Dangerous, Dangerous, Dangerous!

Get the message?
It should be very clear.

Denisev Martinez

If a Person Supports a Group

Trawley Harper

If a person supports a group,
Let that person support that group.
We and that person that supports that flag,
Are two different persons.
And ya you know what I mean.

That flag means something to them.
But that flag might not mean anything to you.
But on the other hand that flag
Might support something that
You don't like or support.

But at the end,
You can't change their mind.
That's ok, just let them.

Mely Flores

Buy, Buy, Buy!

Trawley Harper

BUY, BUY, BUY!
Come on, don't be surprised!
Just take a look and stop by,
Come on, you 're a good guy!

BUY, BUY BUY!
Our food is the best,
Don't tell me lies!
You can even randomize.

BUY, BUY, BUY!
Our food is so tasty,
You will never be hasty!

BUY BUY BUY!

Mely Flores

Vote!

Trawley Harper

Vote! If you don't, no one will be safe.
Vote! If you don't, people could lose their jobs.
Vote! If you don't, it will be your fault
That we get overrun buy problems.

Vote! You could be the reason
Someone is homeless.
Vote! Don't you want to
Have your opinion be the tie-breaker?

Vote! You don't want to be
The reason our economy collapses.
You can help.
You can be the change.

You can be the reason we survive.
You can be the hope for all of us.
You can vote. We all need to vote.
We all need each other's help to thrive through this.

Vicky Flores

Black Lives Matter

Isabella Giraldo Villegas

"Black Lives Matter!" People are yelling in the street.
"Black Lives Matter!" People are protesting endlessly.
"Black Lives Matter!" People shout at all the policemen.
"Black Lives Matter!" People are holding signs.

"Black Lives Matter!" People are making their voices heard.
"Black Lives Matter!" People yell with all their hearts.
"Black Lives Matter!" People make others understand.
"Black Lives Matter!" People are together now.

"Black Lives Matter!" Hundredths of people say,
No matter the color or race.
"Black Lives Matter!" We are all together in this,
Everyone is human and everyone bleeds.

"Black Lives Matter!"
Black people are equal to everyone else,
They deserve respect and the
Right to express themselves.

Mely Flores

Big Fat Liars

Trawley Harper

My parents are a pair of big fat liars.
They said they would buy me those shoes.
They are still not on my feet.

My parents are a pair of big fat liars.
They said they would buy me the superman figurine.
They are still not on my bed.

My parents are a pair of big fat liars.
They said they would play the game with me.
They are not in my bedroom.

My parents are a pair of big fat liars.
They said they would come back after work.
They are in a long wooden box.
That is not home.

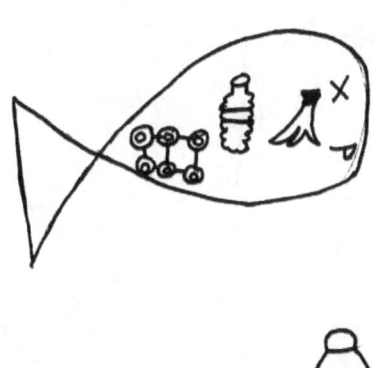

Mely Flores

Join the Club

Brooke Cumbee

They say to dress with oversized clothes
They say to dress with too short clothes
Then they say to wear really fancy clothes
Shouldn't they just choose?

They say to draw on your shoes.
They say to wear just white shoes.
Then they say to wear neon light-up ones.
Why can't we just choose for ourselves?

They change it so much.
But we always follow.
I always follow
Because it seems normal.

Denise Martinez

We're All Doing It

Ryan Chaplin

Come here! We're popular.
Everyone loves our good,
No good products!
You'll like it too!

Check the "stats"
Just like everyone else.
As we expected…
Now we're really #1

Like ants with sugar,
Hamsters with fruit,
Teens with acceptance,
We attract and also chase.
Our #1 way to bait!

Denise Martinez

Chicken Army

Jameson Perkins

Endless possibilities,
Endless things to do,
Endless chickens,
So come and join the chicken army.

Here you'll be given your own chicken,
To train,
Grow,
And take care of

Everyone's joining us,
So you should too,
Come and join us,
At the chicken army.

Mely Flores

You Maybe Missed Out

Issabella Giraldo Villegas

If you haven't heard about Squid Game,
Then you live under a rock!
Squid Game did something surprising,
Becoming the most popular series on Netflix in the world.

Everyone has been watching it during the past month,
And it has been watched massively around the globe.
At least 100 million people have watched this series
And if you don't watch it, you will be left behind
And probably spoiled.

This series is amazing with
Details and surprises, the production is very
Professional and the visual effects seem very real.
This is one of the most original series there

Have ever been, making the viewers feel
Every kind of feeling. Squid Game is an
Extraordinary series, so you better watch it now,
To not feel lonely, left out, or disoriented.

Micayah Seabrook

Everybody Loves It

Trawley Harper

Oh look a new phone, so shiny and cool right?
Everybody loves it.
Everybody will like you.

Oh well, guess I will go buy that phone.
Might get in dept with my bank.
Maybe have to go steal from a few banks.

Who cares? I'll have the cool awesome
Totally amazing new phone!
It's ridiculously expensive, but here we go!

Went bankrupt, broke it the next day.
Awesome phone .

THE NEW SMALL
PETTY

·NOW with 25% more
natural pre-tested products

·GIVES you 75% more
conviced than other perfumes that
said the same thing. (LIED TO YOU!!)
Call Now @ 843-023-6942

Mely Flores

Like a Bee

Josephine Smalls

They all have a fancy car
And you should too.
There is nothing really
Stopping you.

Get a shiny one almost free
Everyone will buzz by you
Like a bee.

If you don't like it,
That's ok.
It might be more expensive
When returned,
But it's worth it.

If you want
A fancy car
Today!

Dinosaurs Are Back!

Dinosaurs Are Back!

Dinosaurs Are Back!

Dinosaurs Are Back!

Dinosaurs Are Back!

Dinosaurs Are Back!

Dinosaurs Are Back!

Dinosaurs Are Back!

Dinosaurs Are Back!

Dinosaurs Are Back!

Dinosaurs Are Back!

Cara Dawn

No, Look Over Here

Arson Clayton

This amazing new car is on sale!
I would definitely buy this.
This car is pink and very new.
Buy it!

This car is amazing.
This very famous person has always loved blue dogs.
Pugs, canines, and chihuahuas.
Trust people named log.

Logs are very important.
Also they are sturdy!
I would definitely recommend buying that pink car.
Pink cars are so cool!
Cars are the new big thing.

N'Dea Greenwood

Something Creeping at You

Monty Don

Something creeping up at you.
Behind you, snooping.
A pretty butterfly flies in front of your face,
Chasing it as everything turns into magic.

People cheering.
A dream come true.
Glitter and sparkles everywhere.
All the attention is on you as that
Shadow is behind you.

Puppet strings.
But why should anyone care?
It's a party with every dessert you'd want.
You are the richest and most
Powerful person in the world here.

Pay no attention to the puppet strings.

Christopher Lopez

I am Just Like Y'all

Jose Aguilar Avila

I know where you are coming from.
I also went through this.
I am just like y'all,
So you can trust me.
Whenever I go out there,
I kept y'all in mind.
I battle for the people.

Some people say, "Oh, he's playing you!"
But keep in mind,
I am as humble as they come.
So remember.
Vote for me as your representative.

Hides fat wads of cash

Ka'Naisha Green

Regular People

Jameson Perkins

I live just like a regular person,
Working hard to get things done,
Making tough choices,
Working late on the job.

See I'm just like you,
I have a voice,
Just like you people,
I want the best for this country.

Obama Clone for President,
In his America, everyone's the same,.
Everyone has a voice.
This message was approved by Obama Clone.

Ka'Naisha Green

Look in a Mirror

Jameson O. Perkins

We are just
Like you.

We have problems
Like you.

We eat
Like you.

We sleep
Like you.

We are citizens
Like you.

That is why
You
Should help us
Win the votes.

Brooke Cumbee

Brooke Cumbee

Brooke Cumbee

Olivia Sumerlin

8 Rhetorical Feels

Being Invisible

Jordan Easley

If I'm invisible,
Then I'm basically invincible.
It's not really intentional,
But I hope it's reversible.

Being invisible,
Is basically being unseeable.
If no one saw me then.
My heart would feel unnoticeable.

A Broken Heart

Javion Rickenbacker

Tears fall down a cold earth face.
Crying in the dark silence no voice,
And a broken heart.
My mood is poking me in too deep.

Sadness, no fears, just tears, my ears,
Are bleeding. Put on headphones.
Loud music. I feel like a broken fuse.
The voices sound like thunder in my ears.

Fake smiles, face faces.
A broken heart needs to get braces.
A dark soul, the voices inside me roar like thunder,
He sits in the dark people still wonder.

Why does his room roar with the thunder?
On stormy days, inside the dark, look
In his soul. He has no heart.
We try to tell him to be happy.

N'Dea Greenwood

Sometimes

Keira Collins

Sometimes I feel alive.
Sometimes I feel happy.
Sometimes I talk.
Sometimes I feel wanted.

But most times I feel empty.
Most times I feel numb.
Most times unaware.
Most times I want to hide,

Unviewable by the horrors.
This world contains for me.
Most times,
I wish I could leave.

Denisev Martinez

Hurt So Much

A'Juanna Shaw-Frasier

It's bad.
I lost my dad in 2012.
I was heartbroken.
It hurt so much because I didn't have a father in my life.

In 2021 I lost my uncle.
It hurt because he was my favorite.
I cried all night asking God why.
When I found out he passed away my heart dropped.

But in January I found out my mom was pregnant.
Then in June, we found out it was a girl.
In August my little sister was born.
I was so happy to be a big sister.

Brooke Cumbee

Calling Names

Brooke Cumbee

You say something different then the rest.
"You're Stupid!"
When you may be right but they don't know that.
You may have never met or spoken to them but still…

Maybe your just saying what you heard but still
"YOUR WRONG!"
And they may be, but with the names...
Civil conversation …… no more.

They are out to spite you.

Micayah Seabrook

Throwing Antics

Sanai' Branton

In a debate you see this happen.
You see this in a argument.
Sometimes when two different
Rival teams go at it, throwing antics,
Making hate posts.
Even resulting in confrontational blows.

A hate poster drawing over Donald Trump's face
Implicating he's a clown. A blog quoting
Kylie Jenner saying, "Kim Kardashian is pure plastic."
Usually it's argumentative and sarcastic.
These are used in debates to make them dramatic.
You may think it's entertaining,
But everything is deeper than we think.
It could lead to protests and riots.

Women are Brave

Sanai' Branton

Women are brave.
Women are bold.
Women should be treated with equality.
Men shouldn't think they have more power.
A women can do anything a man can do.

All men do is wait on a woman's doing and do's.
Some men are really brainless.
They don't know anything.
All they are used for is muscle
They're dumb and dont now how to hustle.
They can never maintain.
Feels like they're just dumb with no brain.

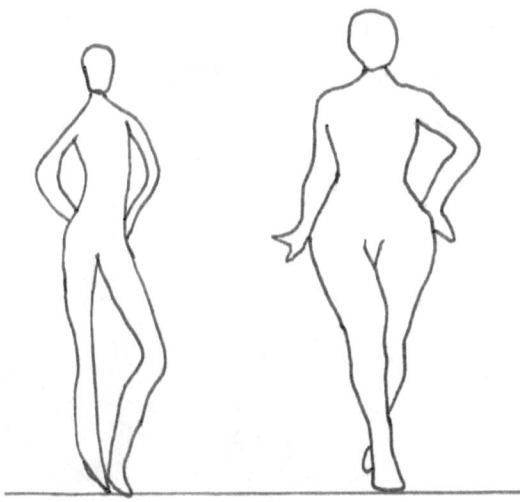

Cara Dawn

Gross

Nathan Jones

McDonalds' chicken is not what you would think.
The clown has been lying to you.
That dumb clown is a disgrace to fast food.
Ronald is not your friend.

Ronald is a scammer.
He doesn't care for his customers.
He uses you for money.
He doesn't care about your health.

He only cares about sales.
Ronald McIdiot is a clown that
Cares only about his well being.
Save yourself from his grip on you.

Stop feeding that idiot money.
It's a waste of your hard earned money.
It is not good for you.
There's no reason to do it.

Denise Martinez

Blabbermouth

Nathan Jones

You are a liar.
You spread fake news.
You are not credible.
You are not a trustworthy person.

You spew lies.
You speak not facts but things that aren't true.
When you speak, you disrespect the founding fathers.
You are a filthy liar.

Please sit down.
Save yourself the embarrassment.
When disrespect the people.
There is no silver lining when you speak.

No one believes you.
Just stop lying.
Liar!
Phony!

Denise Martinez

You are SOOO Lame

N'Dea Greenwood

You are sooo lame.
That's why you don't have fame.
Megan Thee Stallion is doing it.

Join the trend and get popular like her,
But to you, it's just a big blur!
She's gonna notice you.

Just come on.
You're no fun.
It's just a trend come onnnn.

You are being so flam.
Join us!
You will get famous, just like her and us.
Just give me your trust.

Denisev Martinez

Hyperbole

Brooke Cumbee

That one person who is always pointing out.
The smallest thing, and they are always outraged.
Something it does not even involve them,
And they still get involved.
Like, sometimes they need to mind their business.

When they are loud about it,
Like they be making up stuff, too.
Make it sound better for them.
Or when they are making up
Whole stories about people,
And then accidentally tell
The wrong friends about it

They make everything so much bigger.
Sometimes even make things
Worse for themselves.

Like, just calm down,
And stop being so extra.

Mely Flores

Hyperbole

Isabella Giraldo Villegas

"This will make you look 30 years younger!"
Everyone has seen these phrases hundreds of times
In ads, the street, or even in the mall.
But this modern cream is extremely effective,
That it will make you look 40 years younger
And a lot prettier.
This is unbelievable and almost like magic,
If you try it now you will become a crazy fanatic.

Millions of people have tried tons of creams.
With not even a result,
Those people found out,
That the new Cicatricure cream is here to relieve them now.
This gives results in less than a day!
And will make all of the wrinkles quickly fade away.
What are you waiting for?
You should buy the new Cicatricure cream right away!

Ka'Naisha Green

I Saw Angel Numbers

Ryan Chaplin

I saw angel numbers, so I'm blessed.
They are mean because they are a fire sign.
I failed my test because I crossed a pole this morning.
She threw up at church so she's a demon.

They became really sad after listening to heavy metal.
She has good luck because she posts angel numbers.
She's a woman so I believe,
What she has to say about them.

If they don't like math, then they're stupid.
They're blonde, so they're dumb.
He didn't watch barney as a child,
So they had a bad childhood.

If I get a bad grade on this,
Then it's a hate crime.
She lacks creativity,
Because she's a pisces.

Cara Dawn

I'm So Scared

N'Dea Greenwood

I'm so scared
I have nobody to turn to
Who do I call my friend?
I don't know anymore
My "Friends" are trying to kill me
What the heck man
I have nowhere to go
This abandoned house is so scary
I need help out of here
Banging
There it is
Help me
They are coming for me

Ka'Naisha Green

So Save Gas

Jameson Perkins

Here's a family that saves gas,
Notice how they're all happy and alive,
Now here's a family that doesn't save gas,
They're all unhappy and living in terrible conditions.

This is the reason to save gas,
When you do it could save your life,
But also your entries countries,
So save gas.

Because if you don't they'll come,
There bomb the cities of America,
And take everything you have,
So save that gas for the ones overseas.

Because if you don't bad things could happen.

Ka'Naisha Green

Glittering Generalities

Sanai' Branton

Lucky Charms are the best thing in the world.
When you eat them, you spin and grin.
You twirl and swirl.
They make you feel wonderful.

Especially the ones with marshmallows.
They're so good they make your insides feel like jello.
They taste like rainbows and unicorns in your mouth.

They are as sweet as can be.
A really good treat to eat.
They make you want to do nothing but eat them.
Some describe them to be divine.

Christopher Lopez

Humor

Ulises Oliva

I hate math.
First you have to do simple stuff, right?
Add, subtract, multiply, divide.
Then you have to do all four at once?

But only a specific order cause otherwise,
It apparently doesn't want to work.
Then they add letters?!
For real, man, just tell me you have
No clue what it is. Don't add
The alphabet to this crap.

Then they bring in shapes to the mess.
I mean why, do I have to explain how
I know that a triangle is a triangle
With some crazy complex equation
With letters and numbers a Pi.
I was taught what a freaking triangle
Was in 2nd grade, Debra!

And back to Pi. You mean the dessert?
Nope, pi as in that one number with forever or so digits
After the decimal.
Ugh. Math.

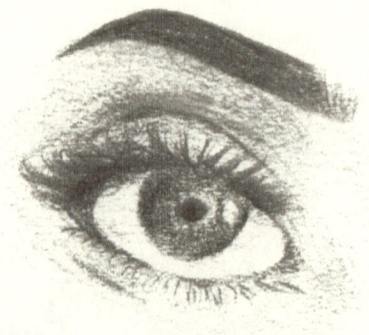
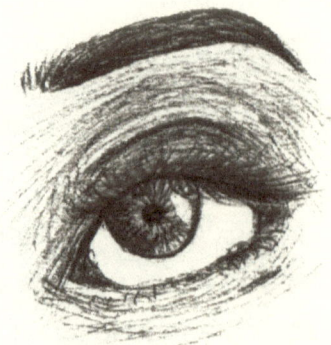

Addis Coronel

Epilogue

Volume 14 is here.

Goodness…is that like twice the lucky 7?

I don't know. Perhaps it is. Maybe it is not.

There's been a lot of changes in the last year. A new principal has come in, new guidance people, new teachers, new students…new everything. We are still trying to figure out the best system for producing the book on time. What an adventure!

This year we managed to add TikTok to our brew of online shenanigans. I am on the fence about this. I know it is all the rage with the teenager types and that adults (including myself) do not understand it, but what the heck. If you don't try, then you don't know. And I still don't know. But the kids are having a good time with it, which counts.

Our Social Media team is doing what they can to increase our online profile. Their efforts are appreciated.

We have another groovy collection of writing and short stories, and artwork from our latest batch of middle school students. As always, there are some jewels in the rough. Our Copy-Editing team diligently works the keyboards to clean up our work and do what they can to select the best of the best. Fantastic!

Support is coming in from the country's far corners, and that is always appreciated. Fundraising remains a challenge, but that's okay. We will get there, one way or another. Our Marketing Team is developing ad campaigns, and we are getting them out to where they need to be and chasing places to sell our wares so we can afford to keep going. Great!

The year started out as they always do. Then, when semester 1 was over, we realized that we hadn't accomplished anywhere near what we needed to accomplish to be ready to publish.

The first team left, and the second team was mostly made up of kids who decided to stay, hit the ground running, and hammered this tome out in record time. We have already started the next one, so we will get both volumes out this year.

What amazes me the most is the kids that remained on our team. They really stepped it up. We have a chance to sell Zuckerbooks at Holy City Brewing's Saturday Market and plan to take that up as soon as the dust settles, so we have that going for us. And the kids who stayed after a lackluster first semester really want to be here and enjoy their work.

Our cover comes from a former student presently attending Kent State University in Ohio – Janell Thomas. It's been years since I've seen her, but a chance passing on our Facebook account connected us, and she was all too happy to send us one of her many collages. It is the first photographic cover, and we are very excited. Thank you, Janell!

This year, happening in the waning months of a pandemic that seems to be without end, has been a challenge. Students are adjusting to returning to in-person learning. Everything seems to be up in the air, including whether or not The Zuckerbook Project will continue to be a class or fade into the history of Zucker Middle School. I guess there's no way to know for sure what will happen, but our plan is, as always, to go out with a bang.

Our greatest challenge?

Paying for producing Zuckerbook, of course. We get donations here and there, but all of our fundraising activities disappeared a year ago, and things are just now coming together on that front. Find us on Facebook and GoFund-Me and donate what you can. Every penny makes a difference.

Believe it or not, the year is still fomenting and coming into its own, so I will have much more for the next Epilogue. Thank you, as always, for reading Zuckerbook.

We do hope you enjoy it.

With gratitude, a tip of the hat, and a big ol' smile,
Erik J. Hilden